WORDSWORTH

CENTENARY STUDIES PRESENTED AT CORNELL AND PRINCETON UNIVERSITIES

WORDSWORTH

CENTENARY STUDIES
PRESENTED AT CORNELL AND
PRINCETON UNIVERSITIES

BY DOUGLAS BUSH, FREDERICK A. POTTLE,
EARL LESLIE GRIGGS, JOHN CROWE RANSOM, B. IFOR EVANS,
LIONEL TRILLING, WILLARD L. SPERRY

EDITED BY GILBERT T. DUNKLIN

PRINCETON, NEW JERSEY
PRINCETON UNIVERSITY PRESS
1951

14323

INTRODUCTION

THIS volume consists of the six lectures on Wordsworth which were delivered at the Wordsworth Centenary Celebrations held at Cornell and Princeton Universities on April 21 and 22, 1950, and Dean Sperry's sermon on Wordsworth's religion which was preached at the Princeton University Chapel on Sunday, April 23, 1950, the one hundredth anniversary of the poet's death. The lectures by Professors Ransom and Trilling were published in the 1950 summer issue of the *Kenyon Review*, and Professor Pottle's lecture appeared in the autumn issue of the *Yale Review*. It is only by coincidence that the essays number seven.

Like other literary anniversaries, the centenary of Wordsworth's death called for recollection, appraisal and revaluation—a critical act performed with distinction by the lectures in this book and by informal exchanges of opinion among the scholars and critics who were invited to attend the Cornell and Princeton meetings. As could be expected, these estimates of Wordsworth's achievement represented different points of view. Sharp disagreements were freely expressed. What readers of Wordsworth have known before—the regrets, vexations, and lassitudes interfused among the finer moments in his poetry—were discussed with a frankness which may have troubled some of the more reverent Wordsworthians. Certainly the occasion honored Wordsworth, and recalled the distinguished studies of his life and works by scholars like Professor Harper and Lane Cooper. But it was not a time of peace, perfect peace. Although the discordant elements may not have been finally reconciled into a calm assurance of Wordsworth's lasting power (which would hardly benefit Wordsworth criticism anyway), the lectures furnished helpful means to the audience—and now to others—for several revaluations of his

v

importance after one hundred years. The order in which the centenary studies are here presented is an attempt to set in balance, and in one kind of continuity, their substantial contributions to a total estimate of Wordsworth's lasting significance.

Professor Bush's "Minority Report" has been given the lead position because it raises the central question, "Is Wordsworth still, for us, a great poet?" Lest there be any doubt as to what is meant by "great" and who is included among "us," some necessary distinctions are made between historical and actual greatness, and a jury is named: the modern critic, the poet, and the general reader "who takes poetry seriously." Mr. Bush advances evidence that all three have found Wordsworth irrelevant and insignificant. The reason is more than an incompatibility growing out of historical developments; Mr. Bush points to a deficiency in Wordsworth: a failure to suspect human nature of evil and a disregard of the misery in life which, even as Matthew Arnold recognized, are unrealistic and unhealthy. Wordsworth's fear of the increasing mechanization of society is not forgotten as a necessary warning to his age and ours; his distrust of an exclusively scientific point of view is also still of value. Nonetheless, the remedy that he offered was inadequate and unsound. It would be possible to argue against Mr. Bush that Wordsworth's antidote was not simply the gospel of man and nature which the "Minority Report" suspects, but that Wordsworth was pleading for an awakening, a new awareness (whether by eye or ear or heart) of the things that matter and endure, among them the better nature of man and the joy offered by nature. Mr. Bush speaks of this very awareness in Wordsworth's poetry; he recognizes its value as a poetic theme, but he wonders if it is as communicable as the kinds of experience found in certain other poets. It is not easy to combat the arguments of a minority report which is so persuasive that it may have spoken for the majority. But after reconsidering Wordsworth's achievement historically and comparatively—and with a critical tolerance that welcomes disagreement—Mr. Bush concludes on a more favorable note by proposing a new Wordsworth anthology. Although one might take exception to some of Mr. Bush's earlier comments on individual poems (as in the case of *Michael* or the *Ode*), the suggestions for his anthology are justified by sensitive criticism. With the familiar selecting and discarding process thus completed at the outset, the subsequent lectures, by analysis of Wordsworth's poetical virtues and defects, largely confirm Mr. Bush's choice.

Professor Pottle's lecture, which was delivered at Cornell, intends "to isolate the qualities of Wordsworth's poetry" that are likely "to be apparent to all historical varieties of sensibility." The aim of "The Eye and the Object in the Poetry of Wordsworth" is "descriptive" rather than "judicial," and its method is to advance by way of two famous statements from the 1800 Preface, the one having to do with "emotion recollected in tranquillity," and the other with the poet's looking steadily at his subject. Mr. Pottle discusses the relation of these statements to each other and the contradiction which they seem to involve. For a clearer understanding of their intended meaning, he analyzes the transition from initial experience into final poetic form of the well-known lines beginning, "I wandered lonely as a cloud." Here one finds what is rare in discussions of the romantic theory of imagination: a detailed, perceptive exposition of poetic text in terms of the method of imagination. Many persons, including the modern critics mentioned by Mr. Bush, are inclined to put little trust in Wordsworth's prefatory theorizing about the origin, manner, and aim of poetry; Mr. Pottle's analysis goes a long way toward removing such doubts. His study explains the Wordsworthian "method of transfiguration," and shows how it is the work of the imagination and not the way of Pope. Imagination and fancy, as Wordsworth conceived them, are defined and distinguished, and the relation is established between the religious and imaginative experience. Mr. Pottle again demonstrates the work of the imagination, this time in *The Solitary Reaper,* and he concludes with an illuminating reference to Blake and the things which he, like Wordsworth, hoped to see and make seen. Because of Mr. Pottle's descriptive discussion, one is confident that they are still available to present-day sensibility.

It seemed fitting to offer next Professor Griggs' painstaking study of Wordsworth as seen through Coleridge's eyes. With full documentation Mr. Griggs thoroughly reviews certain aspects of the theory and practice of Wordsworth and Coleridge which were mentioned by Mr. Bush and more extensively analyzed by Mr. Pottle. Moreover, in the evaluation of Wordsworth in 1950, this report, serving as a kind of flashback, reminds us of the still invaluable assessment of Wordsworth by the first of his important critics. In order to clarify Coleridge's view, Mr. Griggs provides a full résumé of the personal and literary relations between the two poets from 1795 to the publication of the *Biographia Literaria.* The author has gone to all the important sources of information for his study, and new material is presented. The extent of Coleridge's Wordsworth-worship is fully revealed, and from this comes a better understanding of his disappointment with *The Excursion.* Among the many aspects of Wordsworth which are here explored is a temperament which could at times be harsh and unsympathetic almost to the point of cruelty; although one may agree with Mr. Bush that the Wordsworth canon unduly neglects the darker and grimmer elements of life, the Wordsworth story, as reviewed by Mr. Griggs at those points where it involved Coleridge, was not without its share of pain and misery. One could argue, of course, that the truth about Wordsworth was not necessarily as Coleridge saw it, but there can be no doubt that this study has truly presented what Coleridge believed.

Professor Ransom's lecture for the celebration at Cornell declares that Wordsworth "was one of the giants." A modern

critic and poet (and thus one whose interest in Wordsworth
Mr. Bush doubted), Mr. Ransom pays tribute to the innovations in poetic theory which were set forth in the Preface.
Coleridge could have said more for them than he did. In such
poems as _Michael, The Solitary Reaper,_ the Lucy poems, and
The Prelude, there is a plain style which is admirable. By
acute analysis of certain passages in the Preface (notably the
Gray sonnet which is quoted there) and some touchstones
from Wordsworth's verse, this essay explains clearly what
Wordsworth had in mind when he advocated the use of "prose-
poetry" diction. There follows a revealing commentary, in
terms of modern critical theory, on the approach to experience
and the poetic devices in which Wordsworth excels. But the
author's "Notes" are not restricted to the poet's technical excellences (which Mr. Bush also praised as being at times of
the highest order); the latter portion of Mr. Ransom's lecture
examines another of Wordsworth's great originalities, "the love
of nature as the poetic theme." What this is and how it may
come about are discussed with reference to the psychology of
Freud, the philosophy of Dewey, and the poetry of Hopkins.
Here Mr. Ransom accepts some of Wordsworth's beliefs,
though with reservations; he regrets the intrusive dogmatizing,
and he reconstructs the stages in Wordsworth's career where,
as Mr. Ransom believes, the poet was as troubled by his doctrine as some of his readers have been. The spiritual dignity
of Wordsworth's experience in nature is given fuller recognition than Mr. Bush allowed, but Mr. Ransom is in agreement
that the foundations of Wordsworth's achievement, whether
in technical excellence or theme, are the short poems which
most perfectly represent the aesthetic experience.

The fifth lecture was delivered at Princeton by Professor
Evans, who also served as Wordsworthian ambassador from
the Grasmere celebration under the direction of Professor
Helen Darbishire and the Trustees of Dove Cottage. With the
consideration of Wordsworth and the European problem of

the twentieth century, several themes of the preceding studies are continued with the variations of occasional disagreement. Mr. Evans discounts the importance of Wordsworth the poetical theorist, and he sets perhaps a lower value than does Mr. Bush on Wordsworth as a constructive thinker. Wordsworth and Coleridge are again compared, but in this instance the difference concerns their poetry rather than their critical views. The essay defines the unique element of Wordsworth's achievement as an "empirical mysticism" (one is reminded of the evaluations by Mr. Pottle and Mr. Ransom), and it examines the ways in which this special approach to experience may have furthered rather than alleviated the cultural distresses of the nineteenth and twentieth centuries. In this context there is allusion to the stubborn reaction of the later Wordsworth, whose point of view, it is suggested, may be explained in part by the influence of Sir George Beaumont. Mr. Evans' remarks provide reasons in addition to those of Mr. Bush for suspecting that Wordsworth's contribution to the nineteenth century was inadequate and unsound; for the twentieth century, however, Mr. Evans believes that the supreme accomplishment of Wordsworth's art is still accessible and necessary. By a moving comparison with the painter Constable, Mr. Evans demonstrates Wordsworth's "mystical faith in life and in its unity," a faith which is still available after all the destruction of two world wars.

Professor Trilling's lecture, "Wordsworth and the Iron Time," is the necessary complement to the discussions of the preceding chapters. In vigorous disagreement with those who stress the non-Christian aspects of Wordsworth's thought, Mr. Trilling determines the several elements in his work which not only can be identified as Christian but also lie at the center of Wordsworth's belief. In accord with Mr. Bush, Mr. Trilling admits that there is incompatibility between Wordsworth and the modern temperament, but he ascribes this lack of sympathy to Wordsworth's being for us "too Christian a poet"—a point of view quite opposed to the one advanced by Mr. Bush in the opening lecture. Moreover, Mr. Trilling finds a Judaic quality in Wordsworth which has also made him "unacceptable to the modern world." The descriptive analysis of this second characteristic involves an illuminating discussion of what in the *Aboth* is similar to certain elements that are fundamental in Wordsworth's poetry. Special attention is given to Wordsworth's "quietude"; with abundant reference to the trend of Western culture since Wordsworth's time, Mr. Trilling contrasts this element of calm with its opposites by which we have come to live. Similarly, he comments on the Wordsworthian reverence for things of the common life and how this humble piety differs from the modern "passion for the heroic ultimate." Illustrations for his arguments are drawn from the poetry and fiction of Europe and America during the last century, and in this way Mr. Trilling's study, together with those which preceded it, rounds out the full perspective necessary for an evaluation of Wordsworth after one hundred years.

Finally Dean Sperry's sermon on Wordsworth's religion forms the conclusion to this book as it did to the Princeton Centennial. The sermon argues briefly but with authority against some widely held opinions about Wordsworth's beliefs (there is disagreement with Mr. Bush and Mr. Ransom on certain points), and it especially cautions against any identification of Wordsworth's religion with either pantheism or a "sheer quietism." Citing familiar passages of the Wordsworth text, Dean Sperry shows how the poet's religion evolved through the basic stages of all great religious conceptions: the Wordsworthian "solitariness" (which Mr. Pottle referred to as so favorable to the exercise of the imagination) is given new significance for the poet's religion, and then Dean Sperry retraces the Wordsworthian dialectic which culminated in a powerful and positive faith.

The last phrases of the concluding study are a moving reminder of Wordsworth's trust in things to come, and it seems appropriate for the poet as well as for the revaluation of his art that this memorial volume should thus end on a note of assurance. Though Wordsworth was often unreasonably sensitive to any adverse criticism of his poems—even when it was offered by his close friends—it is possible that the ordeal by criticism to which he is here subjected would not have been entirely unwelcome to him. After all, his own assurance of his powers, his faith and his hope, strong though they finally were, grew out of and by the constant testing of inner examination, external accident, the passing of time, and the rites of remembrance. Such trials resemble in function and method the Wordsworth studies which follow, and one may suppose that what in them is adverse to Wordsworth is as necessary for him now as ever, that it will serve him as well in time to come as what is more prompt to encourage his fame. Perhaps in this way the discordant elements will ultimately be reconciled.

G. T. D.

ACKNOWLEDGMENTS

ACKNOWLEDGMENT for permission to quote from their publications is made to the following: Constable & Co., Ltd. (*Coleridge's Miscellaneous Criticism*, edited by T. M. Raysor); J. M. Dent and Sons Ltd. (*Henry Crabb Robinson on Books and Their Writers*, edited by E. J. Morley); Harcourt, Brace and Company (*The Cocktail Party*, by T. S. Eliot); Houghton Mifflin Company (*Letters of Samuel Taylor Coleridge* and *Anima Poetae*, edited by E. H. Coleridge); the Jewish Institute of Religion (*Pirke Aboth*, edited by R. Travers Herford); The Macmillan Company (*Religion in the Making* and *Science and the Modern World*, by A. N. Whitehead; *Form and Style in Poetry*, by W. P. Ker; *The Journals of Dorothy Wordsworth*, edited by E. de Selincourt); The Clarendon Press (*Biographia Literaria*, by S. T. Coleridge; *The Early Letters of William and Dorothy Wordsworth*, edited by E. de Selincourt; *The Letters of William and Dorothy Wordsworth: The Middle Years*, edited by E. de Selincourt; *The Letters of William and Dorothy Wordsworth: The Later Years*, edited by E. de Selincourt; *The Poetical Works of William Wordsworth*, edited by E. de Selincourt and Helen Darbishire); Charles Scribner's Sons (*William Wordsworth*, by George McLean Harper); Sheed and Ward (*Religion and Culture*, by Christopher Dawson); *Times Literary Supplement* and Mr. Nicholas F. D. Coleridge (for a letter in the July 3, 1948 issue).

WORDSWORTH

CENTENARY STUDIES PRESENTED AT
CORNELL AND PRINCETON
UNIVERSITIES

WORDSWORTH:
A MINORITY REPORT

$\mathbb{W}$ HEN I received the pleasant invitation to participate in the centenary celebrations for Wordsworth, I felt even more than the usual need of weighing my capacities. I remembered the shock I long ago gave a fellow graduate student when he discovered that I did not know the color of daffodils; it had been vain to declare that I had a quite satisfactory vision of flowers dancing in the wind, without any color at all. The invitation from Princeton came to me during my first summer on a farm in Vermont, and I hoped that the Green Mountains might bring about the redemption of Peter Bell. However, though there were plenty of old gray stones on which to dream the time away, I sat on a stepladder with a can of paint; I could not reap the harvest of a quiet eye because my eyes were swollen with hay fever; I could not slake my thirst at every rill because our two springs had been condemned by the state laboratory; instead of cuckoos and skylarks singing outside, we had bees and hornets buzzing in the kitchen; instead of

> The silence that is in the starry sky,
> The sleep that is among the lonely hills,

we were kept awake through the night by a neighbor's horses trampling and snorting under our window. Little I saw in nature that was mine. And I thought of the devout Matthew Arnold's admission that Wordsworth's eyes avert their ken from half of human fate. These remarks are not wholly frivolous.

Everyone knows Benjamin Haydon's account of the immortal dinner at which he had among his guests Wordsworth, Keats, and Lamb, and also an unfortunate Comptroller of Stamps

3

who had craved an introduction to Wordsworth. The worthy official, trying to keep his end up, confounded the company by asking Wordsworth "Don't you think, sir, Milton was a great genius?" whereupon the tipsy Lamb took up a candle and wanted to examine the gentleman's phrenological development. It is fairly obvious that Wordsworth was a great genius, that, historically, he ranks among the first five or six English poets. But after a hundred years one may perhaps venture the question, "Is he still, for us, a great poet?" It may be blasphemy or impudence even to put such a query into words, and many of my hearers, in a state of exemplary sobriety, may wish to examine my bumps. But the question cannot damage Wordsworth, and we may see where it leads us.

Mr. Garrod, I think, once remarked that Wordsworth was Coleridge's greatest work and, like Coleridge's other works, left unfinished. But probably neither Mr. Garrod nor anyone else would deny that, in poetry, Wordsworth was the most germinal force among the romantic poets. It was his share in the *Lyrical Ballads* that inaugurated a poetical and spiritual revolution (*The Ancient Mariner,* though it rose far above most of Wordsworth's contributions, was unique and altogether inimitable). It was Wordsworth who, in that and later volumes, showed that poetry could be written in simple language about ordinary humble life. It was Wordsworth who set forth the romantic religion of nature that was to fill a growing spiritual vacuum; who upheld, against the claims of scientific and logical reason, the higher validity of imagination and intuition; who proclaimed the native grandeur of the human soul, and the soul's affinity with the creative spirit that rolls through all things; who maintained that man may be delivered from the bondage of actuality because he has free access to outward and inward sources of enduring beauty and joy and wisdom. All this and much more was Wordsworth's earnest message to mankind, the illumination that he himself—with the aid of his sister and Coleridge—had won from suffering

4

and disillusionment. And while he was, and considered himself, a teacher, he was also a great artist in words, a poet who,
at his best, has a purity of style that achieves the most difficult
of artistic ends, such perfect communication of the experience
that the verbal medium is almost forgotten. If romanticism was
a great rebirth of the human spirit, and if Wordsworth was
the root and center of English romanticism, an inspirer of
multitudes of readers and of poets as diverse as Keats and
Arnold, how can one raise any question of his greatness?

But in trying to estimate the present worth of any poet who
has long enjoyed the status of a classic, we need at times to
distinguish between historical and actual greatness. Historical
greatness grows like a snowball, through its own momentum.
Once an author is established as a quarry for scholarly research,
all his major and minor writings, all major and minor problems,
are accepted as of almost equal importance; the quest of truth
commonly pushes aside questions of value. It is right that
Wordsworthian specialists should try to ascertain, for instance,
the nature of the poet's reaction to Godwinism in *The Borderers*; but the much larger body of non-specialists are still more
right in regarding *The Borderers* as unreadable. I am not
disparaging scholarship; I am merely remarking that scholarly
activity is no criterion of a poet's actual value.

One might add that it is hard to say how much equipment
is needed by the reader of poetry in general and of Wordsworth in particular. For example, there is the little poem that
contains one of Wordsworth's best-known utterances:

> One impulse from a vernal wood
> May teach you more of man,
> Of moral evil and of good,
> Than all the sages can.

When we read the simple poem as we happen to come on it,
it may appeal to us over-intellectual city-dwellers as a refresh-
ing statement of what we have often felt in escaping from

books of philosophy to the unperplexed beauties of nature. That is the obvious and unhistorical response, and it may be enough. But there was much more in Wordsworth's mind when, with playful exaggeration but fundamental seriousness, he rejected the age-old attempts of ethical philosophy to plumb the nature of man and good and evil and turned for true light to external nature. If we wish to understand him, we must know the development in the seventeenth and eighteenth centuries of scientific rationalism and the "enthusiastic" and "sentimental" reaction against it; we must know Wordsworth's own evolution, his early life among the northern hills, the growth of his passion for nature and of his faith in the common man and in the French Revolution, his loss of faith in the Revolution and his need of something to believe in, his ardent espousal of rationalistic thought, then his strong revulsion from all kinds of doctrinaire intellectualism, and his return to belief in the saving power of nature and man's emotional and imaginative intuition. The more we know of all those things, the better we can understand Wordsworth. At the same time, it must be granted that, in the way of historical and philosophical equipment, Wordsworth demands a good deal less from the reader than do most great poets. If it is axiomatic that the final arbiters of any poet's real value are the body of cultivated readers (from which scholars are not to be excluded), the axiom would seem to be especially true for Wordsworth.

It might be further assumed that literary critics, as the best-informed and most perceptive of general readers, are the natural interpreters of poetry, the natural guides for the public at large. In the nineteenth century the critics were as a rule in more or less accord with their readers and not too far ahead of them to be accepted as guides. During that century Wordsworth was pretty thoroughly assessed by many critics, beginning with Coleridge, and, though some did him no service by making him the builder of a philosophical system, on the whole the estimate was judicious. But for a later and very different age no such estimate remains altogether valid. And while modern scholarship has greatly enlarged and enriched our understanding of Wordsworth, modern criticism does not seem to have been greatly interested or very helpful in the process of revaluation. A few critics, far from exalting Wordsworth into a philosopher, have seen him chiefly as the lover of Annette Vallon; we need not linger with that view. Far more important has been the strong modernist hostility toward romantic poetry and the whole post-romantic tradition. Since romantic poetry was inspired by idealistic faith in man, it has been obnoxious to the age of anxiety; and since it was seldom a texture of intellectual wit and paradox, of ironic and oblique complexity, it has been obnoxious to those critics who identify poetry with the "metaphysical" sensibility and technique. This anti-romantic movement has embraced most of the literary intellectuals in the United States and England. Like earlier reactions, such as that of Wordsworth and Coleridge against the eighteenth century, our reaction has sprung from various causes, but in part—like that of Wordsworth and Coleridge— it has been a defense of the new kind of poetry born of our age. The poets of the nineteenth century, with a few exceptions, have been more or less submerged in the anti-romantic wave. As for Wordsworth, one has the impression that he has suffered less from critical hostility than from critical neglect, and neglect implies that a writer seems to be irrelevant, to lack significance for our time. It does not follow, of course, that Wordsworth is dead because he does not fit the rather narrow critical dogmatism that has been prevalent of late; he may be bigger than the fashionable dogmas. Or, if he does lack significance for us, it may be for different reasons.

We come back then to the general body of readers—never in any age a large body—who take poetry seriously, who read it with their whole being and not merely with detached historical or aesthetic intelligence, who think of it as the record of man's moments of vision, as the distillation of his highest and

7

deepest experience. Without slighting the importance of either knowledge or technical analysis, such readers must ask themselves: "What does Wordsworth now actually mean to me? Do I find myself going back to him continually because he gives the kind of profound stimulus and satisfaction that I want?" This may sound naïve, but it seems to me the prime question that confronts each one of us. And it is not an easy question to answer, not merely because one does not know how other persons feel but because one is not quite sure how one feels one's self. Especially in our profession we grow so used to speaking with catholic authority on any author that it may be hard to distinguish between our public and our private sentiments, or even to be certain that we still have the capacity for private sentiments. Besides, in trying to answer the question for one's self, one cannot get rid of blind spots: I have a suspicion of writers who draw a main part of their spiritual sustenance from nature—a prejudice which in this case may be a quite fatal disqualification.

Wordsworth identified himself, and has always been identified by his readers, with a special message concerning nature's relation to man and man's relation to nature. While his mature experience was a natural sequel to that of his childhood and youth, it was not simply a spontaneous growth; it was a strong and conscious revolt against the scientific view of the world and man. To such temperaments as Wordsworth and Coleridge, it seemed that both the outer and the inner world had been thoroughly mechanized by scientists and psychologists; the physical universe and the soul of man were alike governed by mechanical laws and subject to rationalistic analysis. Wordsworth and Coleridge saw the universe and man as enveloped and interpenetrated by mystery and by the all-comprehending unity of spirit:

> Our destiny, our being's heart and home,
> Is with infinitude, and only there.

8

And one might add the still more familiar lines of *Tintern Abbey*:

And I have felt
A presence that disturbs me with the joy
Of elevated thoughts; a sense sublime
Of something far more deeply interfused,
Whose dwelling is the light of setting suns,
And the round ocean and the living air,
And the blue sky, and in the mind of man:
A motion and a spirit, that impels
All thinking things, all objects of all thought,
And rolls through all things.

Such opposed doctrines were not of course essentially new. In the seventeenth century the mechanistic thought of Descartes and Hobbes had aroused the Cambridge Platonists to assert the active reality and unity of spirit. And by the end of the eighteenth century Newtonian science, which at first had been welcomed by poets, and sensationalist psychology, which at first was welcomed by Coleridge and Wordsworth, had come to seem like mechanistic strait jackets imposed upon the universe and the human soul. In the century or more since Wordsworth and Coleridge died, science has gone infinitely farther than they could have anticipated in mechanizing civilization and the heart of man, and a good deal of modern poetry has carried on a new "romantic revolt" against the claims and the desiccating effects of scientific rationalism. All this being so, it might be supposed that Wordsworth would be the inspiration and tutelary genius of the modern movement, whereas it is clear that he is not, that he has meant very little to most modern poets. And what of the common reader, who nowadays is more conscious than ever before of the antagonism between science and any kind of religious or semi-religious idealism? He would be glad to have Wordsworth as a great ally, but does he turn to Wordsworth's faith in the spiritual power of

9

nature and the deep illumination and joy that it offers to man?
I do not think he does.

No one has ever revered Wordsworth more than Arnold
(who, it has been said, had a tendency to regard himself as
Wordsworth's widow), and no one wrote more earnestly of
the poet's "healing power":

> He too upon a wintry clime
> Had fallen—on this iron time
> Of doubts, disputes, distractions, fears.
> He found us when the age had bound
> Our souls in its benumbing round;
> He spoke, and loos'd our heart in tears.
> He laid us as we lay at birth
> On the cool flowery lap of earth;
> Smiles broke from us and we had ease.
> The hills were round us, and the breeze
> Went o'er the sun-lit fields again:
> Our foreheads felt the wind and rain.
> Our youth return'd: for there was shed
> On spirits that had long been dead,
> Spirits dried up and closely-furl'd,
> The freshness of the early world.[1]

These lines, written in April 1850, express what Arnold felt
that he and his age owed to Wordsworth. Almost thirty years
later, in the essay that prefaced his anthology, Arnold delivered
the verdict that Wordsworth was, and would remain, the
greatest English poet after Shakespeare and Milton, and that
he was superior to all modern continental poets, because the
ample body of his poems, especially the many good short
ones, were "superior in power, in interest, in the qualities which
give enduring freshness, to that which any one of the others
has left." But we may think that Arnold the semi-official critic
was farther removed from his own deepest experience and

[1] *Memorial Verses*, 42-57.

convictions, and from ours, than Arnold the poet had been. Arnold's poetry in general is a troubled testimony that Wordsworth's healing power was not enough. Empedocles, the despairing representative of the restless and ruthless modern intellect, looked back with longing, as Arnold looked back to Wordsworth, upon that time when

> we receiv'd the shock of mighty thoughts
> On simple minds with a pure natural joy,

but he could only think of it as gone forever. Empedocles, or Arnold, saw no hope of man's regaining the capacity for simple, natural feeling that belonged to the youth of the race and the youth of the individual. Even the memorial tribute I quoted is a tacit admission that the poet of nature did not meet but withdrew from the problems of the modern mind. And, not to cite further evidence, Arnold made the plain statement with which we began, that

> Wordsworth's eyes avert their ken
> From half of human fate.

In other words, the poet's trust in nature, his trust in feeling, his hopefulness and joy, grew out of a temperament and out of circumstances which slighted the darker and grimmer elements in life, the miseries that flesh and mind are heir to, the high proportion of unhappiness in human existence. If in the middle of the nineteenth century the

> priest to us all
> Of the wonder and bloom of the world

could no longer relieve the spiritual distresses of the modern mind (not to mention other kinds of trouble), what can be said in the middle of the twentieth, when the world and man have gone so much farther into the sandy desert that Arnold so clearly saw, when science has become the dominant religion, when naturalistic and positivistic philosophy has made the general mind distrustful of everything except the empirical fact? Even if we grant that Wordsworth's rejection of rigorously mechanistic thought was essentially right (though it took science a long time to reorientate itself), it might still be said that his peculiar faith in nature evaded rather than transcended scientific rationalism. It could not and did not survive among his immediate poetic disciples, or indeed for himself.

At this point it might be well to anticipate one possible objection by recalling the famous passage on science in the Preface to the second edition of *Lyrical Ballads*:

"Poetry is the first and last of all knowledge—it is as immortal as the heart of man. If the labours of Men of science should ever create any material revolution, direct or indirect, in our condition, and in the impressions which we habitually receive, the Poet will sleep then no more than at present; he will be ready to follow the steps of the Man of science, not only in those general indirect effects, but he will be at his side, carrying sensation into the midst of the objects of the science itself. The remotest discoveries of the Chemist, the Botanist, or Mineralogist, will be as proper objects of the Poet's art as any upon which it can be employed, if the time should ever come when these things shall be familiar to us, and the relations under which they are contemplated by the followers of these respective sciences shall be manifestly and palpably material to us as enjoying and suffering beings. If the time should ever come when what is now called science, thus familiarised to men, shall be ready to put on, as it were, a form of flesh and blood, the Poet will lend his divine spirit to aid the transfiguration, and will welcome the Being thus produced, as a dear and genuine inmate of the household of man."

Wordsworth's prophecy sounds brave and reassuring, but it was to prove no more accurate than prophecies generally do.[2] His conception of nature, the main basis of his faith and

[2] Parts of this paragraph are borrowed from *Science and English Poetry*, by Douglas Bush, New York, 1950.

his poetry, was hardly compatible with biology and the struggle for existence. Moreover, he could not foresee what a multiplied menace even machinery and gadgets were to become—the change, to go no further, from the surrey with the fringe on top to the sound of horns and motors in the spring. Wordsworth did see the rapacious commercialism and the spiritual debasement that accompanied the Industrial Revolution, but he could not foresee that science was to alter the whole tempo and quality of human life and thought and feeling, that it was to change not only the face but the soul of civilization and even threaten its survival. In a word, he dreamed of the humanizing of what was to grow more and more inhuman. That is not, certainly, a charge against Wordsworth in himself and in his own time, but it does have some bearing on Wordsworth in 1950. Since he, so to speak, offered a reply and an antidote to science, it is surely permissible to consider if the antidote was adequate. I do not of course mean to imply that a poet may not hold a belief or idea unless it is sanctioned by science, which operates on another level and has often been dogmatically wrong anyhow, but only that there are some hard facts which imaginative intuition cannot override or ignore.

In answer to these various large questions, many things might be said: that Arnold was only a single disconsolate voice, not an oracle for his own age or ours; that Wordsworth was not a primitivistic escapist and did not avert his eyes from human suffering, but fully recognized the common lot; that he remains a light and a stay for a multitude of modern readers; that, even if he does not, the fault is much less in him than in the temper of an especially troubled age; that science and positivistic thought, however dominant and arrogant, have not extinguished and cannot extinguish the life of the spirit, the human affections, the admiration, hope, and love by which we live; and that in any case the power of great poetry does not depend on the validity of the beliefs and ideas expressed

13

by the poet (who is not a philosopher), but on the total experience we receive from reading him.

Most of these questions and answers are endlessly debatable, and I can only offer some highly debatable comments. Whether or not Wordsworth is actively cherished by a large number of modern readers I do not know, since one cannot sit down at the telephone and inquire, "Have you a book? What poet are you now reading?" So that question must be passed by. In regard to the validity and importance of a poet's philosophy, some readers and critics would deplore any emphasis on what a poet believes and says, and would insist that Wordsworth is entitled to the diplomatic immunity we freely grant to other and older poets who are still alive for us—the Greeks and Romans, Dante and the Christian poets of the English Renaissance from Chaucer to Milton. Well, granted that poetry is an aesthetic experience, it seems to me that unless it ministers, in more than aesthetic ways, to what used to be called our souls, there is not much reason for its being read or written. And I do not think that we common readers are able, even if we wish, to maintain an equal degree of receptivity, or an equally willing suspension of disbelief, toward all kinds of creeds; our knowledge and experience and individual temperaments make some congenial and some not. When we read the Greeks and Romans we may be conscious of being in a pagan and alien world, but we are also conscious of universal human values and, in some poets, of a view of life that is religious by any standard. As for the Christian poets, from Dante to Milton, we may or may not share the chief articles of their religious creed, but—to put the matter in its lowest terms—that creed is at least in our bones. It has the traditional dignity and authority of the greatest of historic religions, and—what is more important—it remains the highest inspiration and criterion of our own religious and ethical gropings because its recognition of what is evil and what is good, of the conflict between the natural and the supra-natural, between pride and humility, remains, even for many non-believers, the most penetrating revelation or insight that man has attained concerning his own nature. But I think that some basic beliefs of Wordsworth, whether we call them pantheism or primitivism, a private myth or auto-intoxication, or whether we use more laudatory names, are more alien to us, less realistic and less satisfying, than those of the pagan or the Christian poets.

In Wordsworth's gospel of nature and man the dualism of both classical and Christian ethics was pretty much dissolved. That fact might validate it for our naturalistic age, but naturalistic thinkers would probably boggle at Wordsworth's faith in the instinctive goodness of man and the inspiring goodness of nature. That Wordsworth's optimistic and humanitarian faith in man has a foundation of doubtful solidity and breadth I think is true. If recent poets and writers in general have been too much inclined to despair, Wordsworth can be charged with a partial view of the opposite kind. In saying that—not that it is a novel opinion—one may of course be an unwitting victim of the partial view characteristic of our melancholy time. But a similar conclusion might emerge from a comparison of Wordsworth with those poets who have most nearly arrived at a comprehensive view of human nature and experience. It would be unfair to Wordsworth, as it would be to most poets, to appeal to the greatest Greeks, or to Lucretius and Virgil, or to Dante and Shakespeare; but no one could object to a comparison with Spenser and Milton or the lesser Chapman and Greville, and I would submit that these and other classical-Christian poets of the Renaissance—whatever their varying poetic power—share a larger, more central, more realistic, and more permanently valid comprehension of the facts of human nature and human life. Wordsworth, like the other romantic poets, stood more or less outside Christianity and had to find a religion for himself; also, he inherited the sentimentalism of the eighteenth century. Though he gave it his own elevated complications and refinements, there was not much room in

15

that doctrine for the sobering conception of man as fallen. If anyone asks, in astonishment, "Why should there be?" it might be said that a conviction of sin is likely to be more conducive to spiritual health than impulses from a vernal wood. One of the chief penalties that attend Wordsworth's kind of thought and feeling—as we see also in Emerson and others—is the loss or attenuation of the sense of evil, the tragic sense. What Wordsworth mourned in *Tintern Abbey* and *Intimations of Immortality* was, to be sure, the loss of what he had lived by, but that was the capacity for sensuous and emotional response to nature.

I am not forgetting that he wrote, with moving power and beauty, of

> the heavy and the weary weight
> Of all this unintelligible world,

though I cannot remember many great poems in which these words find a substantial "objective correlative." I am not forgetting, either, the painful reality of the struggles through which Wordsworth arrived at his belief in nature's beneficent ministry to man. I am only asking if we, who are more concerned with his poetry than his biography, can find there, not merely solace, but a realistic and sustaining consciousness of what we may call the human predicament, or, if you like, original sin. *Intimations of Immortality*, beautiful as it is, records a very individual kind of depression and a very individual solution. The loss that Wordsworth felt so intensely is not one that many people can share, nor is the positive gain in which he rejoiced—since our primal sympathy with man is rarely a compensation for our failing responsiveness to nature. And the passage on the six-year-old child as "Mighty Prophet! Seer blest!" is so unreal a fantasy that it may almost vitiate the whole. When we think of Henry Vaughan's *The Retreat*, we must—even if we say Vaughan's Christian faith was no more "authentic" than Wordsworth's pseudo-Platonism—we must admit that Vaughan's celebration of childish innocence, his grief for sin, and his longing for the pure light of heaven have a more than private validity. If these few remarks are distressingly flat-footed and blind, I can only say that I am not unaware of several recent, sympathetic, and admirable expositions of the ode, Mr. Trilling's among them.[3] And I might add that I would not go nearly so far as Mr. Fairchild in his formidable arraignment of the romantic poets.[4]

As Wordsworth's mythical or mystical view of nature was largely the creation of his own mind, so in a considerable degree his view of man was a mental abstraction or idealization rather imposed upon than drawn from flesh-and-blood humanity. He has a fair amount of poetry or verse about deserted mothers and their offspring, but that theme is not quite a major segment of normal experience. Nor is Wordsworth's abstract vision of life greatly broadened or deepened in other "objective" poems from *Guilt and Sorrow* to *Michael*; with all its beauty and pathos *Michael* is a simple pastoral. How often, we might ask, does Wordsworth make us feel "the fierce dispute Betwixt damnation and impassion'd clay?" To quote Keats is to recall the famous letter in which he said, among other things, that Milton's "Philosophy, human and divine, may be tolerably understood by one not much advanced in years," and that Wordsworth had penetrated more deeply into the human heart.[5] The latter opinion may be true, but Keats shows no sign of having understood *Paradise Lost* apart from its aesthetic qualities, and Milton's central consciousness of the war between good and evil in the world and in the soul of man seems to me to leave Wordsworth nowhere—unless we take in *The Excursion*, and most people do not regard it as an active part of the canon. In short, the ethical Wordsworth tends to

[3] *The Liberal Imagination,* New York, 1950, 129-59.
[4] *Religious Trends in English Poetry, Volume III: 1780-1830,* New York, 1949.
[5] Letter to John Hamilton Reynolds, May 3, 1818.

see man with the somewhat blurred or far-sighted eyes of the mystical Wordsworth. The world of reflection and intuition in which he lives does not except at moments coalesce with our world. To our questionings about man in the universe, man in society, or even man in solitude, Wordsworth does not give much help toward an answer, or toward a realization of the problems.

It may be said, with indignation, that we have no right to expect such help from a poet. But as long as poets speak, and use words that have a meaning, I think we may ask what they mean and where their meaning stands in our scale of values—always remembering, as I hope I am, that we are not judges interpreting a fixed constitution, but that we read poetry because it purifies and enriches our values. It is obvious that Wordsworth's insights came rather from observation of his conscious and unconscious self than from observation of people, that a very high proportion of his writing was a record of his own inner history, his own feelings. He did not, like Chaucer or Shakespeare or Milton, lead the life of a man among men; he was for the most part a brooding recluse, wholly devoted to poetry. And it does not appear that he was actually very intimate with the kind of rural folk he sometimes wrote about, or a very close observer of nature. He was an intensely subjective and introspective poet who had received an illumination that he had to express; but, as I have said, it was a very individual and peculiar illumination, which few can share except in its elementary phases, and which, for Wordsworth himself, excluded large areas of life. He thought of his main theme as "man, the heart of man, and human life," and doubtless many readers would warmly endorse that claim; and some would say, in the up-to-date language of psychology, that the poet created authentic myths and dealt with important states of mind. It seems to me that his main theme of contemplation was not so much man and nature but himself contemplating man and nature. That was not an unimportant subject, but

18

has it a breadth and depth and concreteness that we in our altered world can recognize and respond to? Is Wordsworth's presentation of his experience of reality and man confined in general too closely to the terms of his personal creed to transcend it, to carry those larger implications that make poetry universal? Although Wordsworth's personal beliefs may be less remote from ours than Mr. Eliot's, are we moved by most of his poetry as we are by *Four Quartets?*

So far we have been concerned with the Wordsworth of the great decade, who has always been *the* Wordsworth. But if it is improper to question the ethical value of impulses from a vernal wood, it would be still worse not to remember that the poet himself, through much of that decade, was led to increasing questioning of spontaneous impulse and to increasing acceptance of inward discipline and order, to a new vision of reality. One early product of such a mood was *Resolution and Independence.* Two years later came the very explicit *Ode to Duty,* in which, with a nostalgic tribute to those whose spontaneous love and joy are an unerring light, Wordsworth recognizes his need of a stronger control than blind trust in feeling. And then, in the *Character of the Happy Warrior* and *Elegiac Stanzas,* his embracing of the law of reason and conscience was emotionally strengthened by grief for the death of his brother —"A deep distress hath humanised my soul." The word "humanised" seems to imply an admission that there had something inhuman in his detached serenity, and that the religion of nature was no very sure support against the real sorrows of mankind. We cannot pursue Wordsworth's ethical development through further poems, including *The Excursion,* and can only say that his half-Stoic, half-Christian appeal to self-discipline was the transitional stage between his earlier trust in pure feeling and his later more or less orthodox Christianity. But there is again the fact that "the poetry of Wordsworth" means, with a few exceptions, the poetry of his happy faith in nature and man; and some readers, even devout ad-

19

mirers, so dislike the *Ode to Duty, Laodamia*, and similar
poems that they would say Wordsworth had only put off the
old man to put on the old woman. Whatever his poetical fate,
it does not seem necessary to conclude, for poets in general,
that the attainment of moral wisdom means the end of poetry.
As regards Wordsworth himself, the poetry of his great decade
might have been greater if more of it had been born of conflict
between the ideals of "unchartered freedom" and order. As
it was, much of the poetry we have cherished was the out-
pouring of a too simple harmony of soul.

If Wordsworth is not an active force in our time (and the
mainly negative evidence suggests that he is not), we have
looked at some of the possible reasons, especially what may be
thought the nebulous quality of his mysticism and of his sentimental ethics, and the really very limited range of experience
that he explores. Most or all of what I have said may be quite
wrong-headed—though I did not fully realize when I began
to take stock of my opinions that I was cast for the sour role
of devil's advocate or counsel for the prosecution. However,
Wordsworth is not likely to be injured, and mine may be a
felix culpa if it arouses ardent opposition. I shall gladly be a
martyr in so good a cause—provided that those who kindle
the fire will take oath that the poetry of Wordsworth is one of
their most frequent and precious companions. In going further
than I expected to in discussing possible barriers between
Wordsworth and us, I have not, I may say, given an altogether
fair account of even my own reactions, and the balance cannot
be redressed in a limited space. But I should like to make a
beginning.

If we common readers were compiling our own Wordsworth
anthology, it would probably be a much smaller selection than
Arnold made or than textbooks offer. There are many short
poems, such as those addressed to flowers and birds, which
make pleasant reading but which I at least could spare. We
must have a few of the narrative and reflective poems, and of

course *Tintern Abbey* and *Intimations of Immortality*. We probably read *The Prelude* more as a document than as a poem, and the choice of passages would have to be left to individual discretion; but one might venture to ask if more than fractions of the work can be called great poetry. *The Excursion*—which, I may remark, I have gone through much oftener than Francis Jeffrey and most modern readers—yields a few fine bits, such as that on the Greek religion of nature and some on reason and discipline. And the shorter poems on this last theme, which were referred to before, I should keep, not without misgivings as to whether Wordsworth's "new light" is always carried alive into the heart by passion.

For the rest, the poetry that seems to me the finest, that speaks to us most directly, is mainly of two kinds. One kind or group comprises some short poems in which nature is subordinated to humanity and in which there is little or no philosophizing. Of these *The Solitary Reaper* might stand as a perfect example. Here the slightest of rural incidents, which could have occurred in any country in any age, is not artificially heightened but simply realized, with a power of verbal and rhythmical suggestion that is at once homely and rich, concrete and magical. And to that may be added some other pieces of similar timeless and "commonplace" universality, such as the best of the Lucy poems.

The other group embraces a good many of the sonnets, those on Milton, on British ideals of the past and sins of the present, on Toussaint L'Ouverture, and kindred subjects, and some on various themes, from the sight of London at sunrise to mutability. In the public sonnets Wordsworth speaks, not with the voice of a bird-watcher, but in the ringing tones of a man among men, a man whose magnanimous idealism and profound anxiety entitle him to deal with nations and great events. Whatever the poet's debt to Milton, this poetry springs from real conflict and has massive strength. In these heroic sonnets, and in others of quieter nobility, Wordsworth is in line with the great poets back through Milton to the ancients. Because he has here a sober consciousness of the facts of human nature and life, he earns the right to celebrate man's unconquerable mind; he does make us feel that we are greater than we know. And perhaps our small anthology holds enough to carry Wordsworth through another hundred years.

THE EYE AND THE OBJECT
IN THE POETRY OF WORDSWORTH

BY FREDERICK A. POTTLE

A CENTENARY year invites the publication of a great many essays with some such title as "Wordsworth Today." The purpose of these essays would be to judge Wordsworth as though he were a contemporary poet, to decide what portion of his works is really available to present-day sensibility. My purpose in the remarks that follow is descriptive rather than judicial: I shall try to isolate qualities of Wordsworth's poetry that look as though they were going to be apparent to all historical varieties of sensibility, though the values assigned to them by different sensibilities may differ. And I think I can best get to what I want to say by the method of texts: by inviting you to consider two prose statements made by Wordsworth himself about poetry in general and about his own poetry in particular. They are both from the famous Preface: "Poetry takes its origin from emotion recollected in tranquillity" and "I have at all times endeavoured to look steadily at my subject." It is my notion that the latter of these texts usually gets, if not a false, at least an impoverished, interpretation; and that the two, taken together and rightly understood, go a long way toward placing Wordsworth in literary history.

At first sight it looks as though they were what Bacon calls "cross clauses": that is, they appear to be hopelessly contradictory. The natural image that rises in one's mind as one reads the statement "I have at all times endeavoured to look steadily at my subject" is that of an artist painting from a model or an actual landscape; and since Wordsworth's poetry contains a good deal of landscape, the obvious meaning of his words would appear to be that he composed poetry while looking earnestly and steadily at the natural objects that he introduces

into his poems. But if poetry takes its rise from "emotion recollected in tranquillity," it is hard to see how this can happen.
In fact, the only way in which we can leave any place for the
actual model, in poetry that starts from recollection, is to suppose that after poetry *has* taken its rise, the poet goes back to
natural objects and pores over them as he composes. And we
know that Wordsworth did not do that. His normal practice,
like that of other poets, was to paint without the model. He
very seldom made a present joy the matter of his song, but
rather turned habitually for the matter of poems to joys that
sprang from hiding-places ten years deep.

More than that, a good many of his poems, including several
of his finest, either have no basis in personal experience at all,
or show autobiography so manipulated that the "subject" cor-
responds to nothing Wordsworth ever saw with the bodily eye.
His extensive critical writings deride the matter-of-fact and
speak over and over again of the power of the imagination to
modify and create. Yet there is a widespread belief that Wordsworth was Nature's Boswell, in the old erroneous sense which
defined Boswell as a man who followed Johnson about with a
notebook, taking down his utterances on the spot. Actually, like
Boswell, Wordsworth relied on memory, and says so quite explicitly. But then he says other things in which he appears to
be vindicating the rightness of his poetry, not on the ground
that it is well-imagined, but on the ground that the things described in the poem really did happen in that fashion and in no
other. I do not mean merely the notes which he dictated in old
age to Miss Fenwick. There is his impassioned defense of *The
Leech Gatherer* against the mild and sisterly strictures of Sara
Hutchinson, a defense made before the poem was published:
"A young Poet in the midst of the happiness of Nature is described as overwhelmed by the thought of the miserable reverses
which have befallen the happiest of all men, viz Poets—I think
of this till I am so deeply impressed by it, that I consider the
manner in which I was rescued from my dejection and despair

almost as an interposition of Providence. . . . 'A lonely place, a Pond' 'by which an old man *was,* far from all house or home' —not stood, not sat, but *'was'*—the figure presented in the most naked simplicity possible. . . . I cannot conceive a figure more impressive than that of an old Man like this, the survivor of a Wife and ten children, travelling alone among the mountains and all lonely places, carrying with him his own fortitude, and the necessities which an unjust state of society has entailed upon him. . . . Good God! Such a figure, in such a place, a pious self-respecting, miserably infirm . . . Old Man telling such a tale!"[1]

Who would believe from reading this that in real life Wordsworth met the old man, not on the lonely moor, but in the highway; that the old man in real life was not demonstrating resolution and independence by gathering leeches under great difficulties, but was begging? In short, that the narrative is from first to last an imaginative construction—the account of an imagined meeting between Wordsworth and the beggar as Wordsworth imagined him to have been before he was finally reduced to beggary?[2]

What, then, are we to make of Wordsworth's boast that he endeavored at all times to look steadily at his subject? I shall try to answer the question by tracing the steps he followed in writing one of his most famous poems, *I wandered lonely as a cloud,* commonly (though with no authority from Wordsworth) called *Daffodils.*[3] The starting point is the entry in Dorothy Wordsworth's *Journal* for April 15, 1802. That entry is fairly long, but it is all good reading; and I have my reasons for not eliminating any of it:

"It was a threatening, misty morning, but mild. We set off

[1] Letter of June 14, 1802. *The Early Letters of William and Dorothy Wordsworth:* (*1787-1805*), ed. by E. de Selincourt, Oxford, 1935, 305-6.

[2] Dorothy Wordsworth's *Journal,* Friday, October 3, 1800. *Journals of Dorothy Wordsworth,* ed. by E. de Selincourt, 2 vols., New York, 1941, I, 63.

[3] The poem is printed at the end of this essay.

after dinner from Eusemere. Mrs. Clarkson went a short way with us, but turned back. The wind was furious, and we thought we must have returned. We first rested in the large boat-house, then under a furze bush opposite Mr. Clarkson's. Saw the plough going in the field. The wind seized our breath. The Lake was rough. There was a boat by itself floating in the middle of the bay below Water Millock. We rested again in the Water Millock Lane. The hawthorns are black and green, the birches here and there greenish, but there is yet more of purple to be seen on the twigs. We got over into a field to avoid some cows—people working. A few primroses by the roadside —woodsorrel flower, the anemone, scentless violets, straw-berries, and that starry, yellow flower which Mrs. C. calls pile wort. When we were in the woods beyond Gowbarrow Park we saw a few daffodils close to the water-side. We fancied that the lake had floated the seeds ashore, and that the little colony had so sprung up. But as we went along there were more and yet more; and at last, under the boughs of the trees, we saw that there was a long belt of them along the shore, about the breadth of a country turnpike road. I never saw daffodils so beautiful. They grew among the mossy stones about and about them; some rested their heads upon these stones as on a pillow for weariness; and the rest tossed and reeled and danced, and seemed as if they verily laughed with the wind, that blew upon them over the lake; they looked so gay, ever glancing, ever changing. This wind blew directly over the lake to them. There was here and there a little knot, and a few stragglers a few yards higher up; but they were so few as not to disturb the simplicity, unity, and life of that one busy highway. We rested again and again. The bays were stormy, and we heard the waves at different distances, and in the middle of the water, like the sea. Rain came on—we were wet when we reached Luff's, but we called in. Luckily all was chearless and gloomy, so we faced the storm—we *must* have been wet if we had waited—put on dry clothes at Dobson's.

I was very kindly treated by a young woman, the landlady looked sour, but it is her way. She gave us a goodish supper, excellent ham and potatoes. We paid 7/- when we came away. William was sitting by a bright fire when I came downstairs. He soon made his way to the library, piled up in a corner of the window. He brought out a volume of Enfield's *Speaker*, another miscellany, and an odd volume of Congreve's plays. We had a glass of warm rum and water. We enjoyed ourselves, and wished for Mary. It rained and blew, when we went to bed. N.B. Deer in Gowbarrow Park like skeletons."[4]

I said this was the starting point, for it is as near the raw matter of the poem as we can get. The true raw matter consisted of certain perceptions, visual, auditory, tactile, which Wordsworth and his sister had on that windy April morning— and those we have no way of recovering. In Dorothy's entry this raw matter has already been grasped and shaped by a powerful imagination, and it has been verbalized. The entry is not a poem, because it contains a good deal of true but inconsequential statement (the rum and water, the volume of Congreve), but much of it is prefabricated material for a poem. And the fact is (though this is doctrine little heard of among men) that Wordsworth made grateful use of prefabricated material whenever he could get it of the right sort. As Professor Lane Cooper showed us long ago,[5] he went regularly to books of travel for material of the right sort, but his best source was his sister's journal.

The function of the imagination, as Wordsworth and Coleridge insisted, is, at the first level, to make sense out of the undifferentiated manifold of sensation by organizing it into individual objects or things; at the second, and specifically poetic, level, to reshape this world of common perception in

[4] *Journals of Dorothy Wordsworth*, i, 131-2.
[5] "A Glance at Wordsworth's Reading," *Modern Language Notes*, Vol. xxii, Nos. 3 and 4 (March and April 1907), 83-9, 110-17; reprinted with alterations in *Methods and Aims in the Study of Literature*, ed. by Lane Cooper, Boston, 1915.

the direction of a unity that shall be even more satisfactory and meaningful. Dorothy has made extensive use of the secondary or poetic imagination. Notice the devices by which she has unified and made sense of the experience of the daffodils. First, and most important, she has endowed them with human qualities. They are a social group engaged in busy concerted activity. The notion of the social group, the crowd (she does not actually use the word) is reinforced by her further figure of stragglers. Secondly, besides being active, the crowd of daffodils is happy: they look gay, they toss and reel and dance (their very activity is sport) and seem verily to laugh. And thirdly, some of the crowd have danced so hard that they are tired: they rest their heads upon the stones as on pillows.

Wordsworth recollected the scene in tranquillity and wrote his poem a full two years afterwards. He fixes on Dorothy's fine central perception of "the simplicity, unity, and life of that one busy highway," and condenses it into the one word "crowd," which, as we have seen, she did not use. He takes over, too, her impression that the daffodils were "dancing," that they were "gay," that they were even "laughing." Ever since 1807, when Wordsworth published this poem, daffodils have danced and laughed, but there is nothing inevitable about it. The Greek myth of Narcissus is not exactly hilarious; and even Herrick, when he looked at a daffodil, saw something far from jocund:

> When a Daffadill I see,
> Hanging down his head t'wards me;
> Guesse I may, what I must be:
> First, I shall decline my head;
> Secondly, I shall be dead;
> Lastly, safely buryed.

The literal, positivistic, "scientific" fact was that Wordsworth and his sister saw a large bed of wild daffodils beside a lake, agitated by a strong, cold spring wind. The rest is all the work of the imagination.

The mark of the poetic imagination is to simplify: to make the manifold of sensation more meaningful by reducing it to a number of objects that can actually be contemplated. Wordsworth continues Dorothy's process of simplification: he eliminates the bitterness of the wind, which is so prominent in her account; reduces the wind, in fact, to a breeze. It may appear here that he has simplified more than was necessary or wise. Shakespeare, in the most famous lines ever written about daffodils, kept the wind:

> daffodils
> That come before the swallow dares, and take
> The winds of March with beauty.

Admittedly, it is a higher mode. Wordsworth, on some occasions, would have kept the wind, too; but to have kept it here would have made a more complex—if you will, a more tragic—poem than he felt like writing. He felt this poem as something very simple and very pure; when he came to publish it, he put it in a group called "Moods of My Own Mind." But he is impartial: as he throws out matter on the one hand because it is too serious, he throws out matter on the other because it is too playful. The prettiest thing in Dorothy's realization— her image of the daffodils pillowing their heads on the stones —drops out. He dispenses too with Dorothy's stragglers. He fastens on her central image of the dancing, laughing crowd, and lets everything else go.

But now the idea of the crowd calls for a modification, and a modification of a fundamental sort. The social glee of the crowd can be made more significant if it is set over against solitary joy; and so in the poem he makes himself solitary, which in literal fact he was not. He now has what for him is a promising situation. The solitariness of the poet and the sociability of the daffodils are set up as poles between which the poem discharges itself. I have said that the situation is for him a promising one. Everyone knows of Wordsworth's love of solitude, his conviction that the highest experiences came to him when he was alone. What we need constantly to remind ourselves of is that his theory assigned an only slightly lower value to the love of men in societies. (The subtitle of Book VIII of *The Prelude* is "Love of Nature Leading to Love of Man.") The trouble was that, though he had the best of intentions, he could never handle close-packed, present, human crowds in the mode of imagination. If he were to grasp the life of a great city imaginatively, it had to be at night or early in the morning, while the streets were deserted; or at least in bad weather, when few people were abroad.[6] The Seventh Book of *The Prelude* ("Residence in London") is one of the most delightful things Wordsworth ever wrote, but as he himself tells us, it is almost all in the mode of fancy—almost all poetry that groups with *The Kitten and the Falling Leaves.*[7] But in the figure of a bed of daffodils endowed with human characteristics, he can handle with feelings of approval and exhilaration the concept of a crowd, of ten thousand individuals packed close together. He begins and ends solitary: at the beginning, we may assume, filled with joy, but a joy somewhat solemn, somewhat cold and remote, as the symbol of the cloud indicates. He is surprised by the sensation of mere unmixed human gaiety and lightheartedness, yields to it, and finds it good; so good that ever after he can derive refreshment from the memory of the experience.

I ought perhaps to be no more specific, but my purposes demand a somewhat closer analysis of Wordsworth's formal devices. The extension in space which he secures by linking the daffodils to other objects in nature—stars and waves—is characteristic of his poems of the imagination, but I shall defer

---

[6] *The Prelude* (1850), vii, 654-68; *Earth has not anything to show more fair.*
[7] *The Prelude* (1850), vii, 436-41.

discussion of this. The second stanza is ostensibly introduced merely to reinforce the idea of number ("continuous" echoing "crowd" and "host"), but of course there are other meaningful parallels. "Stars" looks back to "golden," and "twinkle" echoes "fluttering."[8] So, too, the third stanza professes only to reinforce the idea of dancing, but actually reinforces also the idea of number (waves are always numberless); and "sparkling" looks back to "twinkle," and back of that to "fluttering." The progress toward explicit identification of the symbol is gradual. First we have "fluttering" (literal: the flowers are moved by the breeze); then "dancing" (the flowers are self-moved); then "tossing their heads in sprightly dance." (The flowers are self-moved and are having a wonderful time. "Dance" is the key word: you will have noticed that it occurs in either the last or the first line of each of the four stanzas.) Finally—but not until the third stanza is reached—we get the quite explicit series "glee," "gay," "jocund," "pleasure." Wordsworth is always (or almost always) explicit in this fashion: he tells you just how you are expected to take his figures. Of course it is the figures that convey the emotion. No one can make us joyful merely by using the word "joy" or any of its synonyms. But there is impressive agreement among readers of all periods that by giving us a simple figure, reinforcing it by certain devices of varied iteration, and explicitly interpreting it, Wordsworth does evoke the emotion of joy.

We can now see what Wordsworth meant by looking steadily at his subject. So far as his subject is expressed in imagery drawn from nature (and that means in all his best poetry), there is implied a lifelong habit of close, detailed, and accurate observation of the objects composing the external universe. By "accurate" I mean something the same thing as "naturalistic," but not entirely so. Wordsworth scorned the merely ana-

[8] The second stanza was added in 1815. To accommodate it, some very skillful changes were made in the first stanza. Line 4 read originally "A host of dancing daffodils" and line 6, "Ten thousand dancing in the breeze."

lytic vision of the naturalist ("One that would peep and botanize Upon his mother's grave") because in his opinion that kind of apprehension empties the object of life and meaning by detaching it from its ground. "His theme is nature *in solido,* that is to say, he dwells on that mysterious presence of surrounding things, which imposes itself on any separate element that we set up as an individual for its own sake. He always grasps the whole of nature as involved in the tonality of the particular instance."[9] But, except for those portions of the scientist's vision which require (let us say) dissection and magnification, there is little in the scientist's vision that Wordsworth misses. A *merely* matter-of-fact, an *exclusively* positivistic view of nature fills him with anger, but his own apprehension includes the matter-of-fact view without denying any of it. Dr. Leavis has perhaps put this more intelligibly when he remarks, as the chief virtue of Wordsworth's poetry, a "firm hold upon the world of common perception,"[10] though I myself should like to phrase it, "in the mode of perception which has been common in Western civilization since some time in the late eighteenth century." In a literal, physiological sense, Wordsworth did look steadily at the natural objects that appear in his poetry.

But the subject he is talking about in the sentence in the Preface is not an object in external nature; and the eye that looks steadily is not the physical eye. The subject is a mental image, and the eye is that inward eye which is the bliss of solitude. The mental image accompanies or is the source of the emotion recollected in tranquillity; it recurs in memory, not once but many times; and on each occasion he looks at it steadily to see what it *means.* Wordsworth in his best poetry does not start with an abstraction or a generalization, a divine commonplace which he wishes to illustrate. He starts with the

[9] *Science and the Modern World,* by Alfred North Whitehead, New York, 1925, 121.
[10] *Revaluation,* London, 1936, 175.

mental image of a concrete natural object. He feels this object to be very urgent, but at first he does not know why. As he looks steadily at it, he simplifies it, and as he simplifies it, he sees what it means. He usually continues to simplify and interpret until the object becomes the correlative of a single emotion. It is a great mistake to consider Wordsworth a descriptive poet. When he is writing in the mode of the imagination, he never gives catalogues, in fact never provides a profusion of imagery.[11] He employs few images. His images are firm and precise ("literal"), but, as one of my undergraduate students acutely said, they are very spare.[12] Of the daffodils we are given nothing but their habit of growing in clumps, their color, and their characteristic movement when stirred by the wind. Wordsworth's method (I am trying to be just as hard-headed and precise as I know how) is not the method of beautification (Tennyson), nor the method of distortion (Carlyle); it is the method of transfiguration. The primrose by the river's brim remains a simple primrose but it is also something more: it is a symbol (to use Hartley's quaint terminology) of sympathy, theopathy, or the moral sense.[13]

We can also see now the main cause of Wordsworth's dissatisfaction with the poetry of Pope: "It is remarkable that, excepting the nocturnal Reverie of Lady Winchilsea, and a passage or two in the Windsor Forest of Pope, the poetry of the period intervening between the publication of the Paradise Lost and the Seasons does not contain a single new image of external nature; and scarcely presents a familiar one from which

[11] E.g., in a poem of the imagination he could have done nothing with Dorothy's pleasant sentence, "A few primroses by the roadside—wood-sorrel flower, the anemone, scentless violets, strawberries, and that starry, yellow flower which Mrs. C. calls pile wort." That would have suited Shelley's mode: see The Question.

[12] He perhaps picked up the adjective from John Crowe Ransom's The World's Body, New York, 1938, 141, though it is there used of the Metaphysicals, not of Wordsworth.

[13] Loving awareness of men ("the still, sad music of humanity"), loving awareness of God ("something far more deeply interfused"), morality ("all my moral being").

it can be inferred that the eye of the Poet had been steadily fixed upon his object, much less that his feelings had urged him to work upon it in the spirit of genuine imagination. To what a low state knowledge of the most obvious and important phenomena had sunk, is evident from the style in which Dryden has executed a description of Night in one of his Tragedies, and Pope his translation of the celebrated moonlight scene in the Iliad. A blind man, in the habit of attending accurately to descriptions casually dropped from the lips of those around him, might easily depict these appearances with more truth."[14] For Pope's usual method is the exact contrary of that which I have been describing. Pope starts with an abstraction or a generalization concerning human nature and then looks for a correlative in the world of nature apart from man. His habit of observation of external nature is not detailed and precise; indeed, he thinks it unimportant whether the "facts" of nature which he alleges in his illustrations are really facts or superstitions. The natural history of Pliny and the old bestiaries are as much grist to his mill as the latest papers of the Royal Society. He appears also to me to have at times no clear, detailed, and consistent mental picture of his own figures. To illustrate: in the couplet near the beginning of the *Essay on Man*,

> The latent tracts, the giddy heights explore
> Of all who blindly creep or sightless soar,

he means, I suppose, moles and birds of some sort. If so, in order to enforce his doctrine that "the proper study of mankind is man," he appears to be making use of the ancient and medieval notion that all birds except the eagle blind themselves by looking at the sun. Surely, by Pope's time it was generally known that the high-flying birds are not "sightless"; that on the contrary they have telescopic vision.

When in the same poem he says that man

[14] Essay, Supplementary to the Preface, 1815.

Touches some wheel, or verges to some goal,[15]

I cannot convince myself that he could draw a diagram of the machine he has in mind. Or consider a famous passage from the Second Dialogue of the *Epilogue to the Satires* (he is referring to satire itself):

> O sacred Weapon! left for truth's defence,
> Sole Dread of Folly, Vice, and Insolence!
> To all but Heav'n-directed hands deny'd,
> The Muse may give thee, but the Gods must guide.
> Rev'rent I touch thee! but with honest zeal;
> To rowze the Watchmen of the Publick Weal,
> To Virtue's Work provoke the tardy Hall,[16]
> And goad the Prelate slumb'ring in his Stall.
> Ye tinsel Insects! whom a Court maintains,
> That counts your Beauties only by your Stains,
> Spin all your Cobwebs o'er the Eye of Day!
> The Muse's wing shall brush you all away.[17]

"Tinsel" to me means "shining or glittering like cheap metal foil,"[18] and my natural image of a "tinsel insect" would be some kind of beetle ("this Bug with gilded wings"). But the word can mean no more than "pretentiously showy" and so may not have been intended to identify the kind of insect Pope has in mind. "Stains," however, can hardly mean anything else than moths or butterflies ("Innumerable of stains and splendid dyes, As are the tiger-moth's deep-damask'd wings"). But the trouble with that is that Pope's insects spin cobwebs, which no butterfly or moth can do. I think we shall do Pope no injustice if we conclude that his insects have the combined

[15] I, 58-9.
[16] Westminster Hall, the hall of justice.
[17] Lines 212-23.
[18] My sense of the word is probably affected by unconscious false etymology: *tinsel* from *tin*. The word is actually derived from French *étincelle*.

characteristics of beetles, moths, and spiders, and hence do not belong to any order known to naturalists.[19]

Looking steadily at a subject, then, for Wordsworth means grasping objects firmly and accurately in the mode of common perception and then looking at them imaginatively. And we have not said all that needs to be said about the second half of the process. I have made a great deal of *I wandered lonely,* and must add now that Wordsworth had doubts about putting that poem in the central group of his short pieces called "Poems of the Imagination." In the collected edition of 1815, where the grouping first appeared, he added the following note to *I wandered lonely:* "The subject of these Stanzas is rather an elementary feeling and simple impression (approaching to the nature of an ocular spectrum) upon the imaginative faculty, than an *exertion* of it."

It is hard for us nowadays to understand why Blake, Wordsworth, Coleridge, and Shelley made such a fuss about the imagination, and why Wordsworth and Coleridge labored so to distinguish the imagination from the fancy. Make no mistake about it: it was for them a matter of vital importance, nothing less than a vindication of their right to exist as poets. In the reigning psychology of Locke extended by Hartley, imagination and fancy—pretty much interchangeable terms—were handled as modes of memory. That in itself was proper enough, but there was a strong tendency to make a total and exclusive philosophy out of this mechanistic naturalism. Wordsworth and Coleridge were convinced that imagination and

[19] "Tinsel," "stains," and "cobwebs" would all be appropriate for certain varieties of spiders, but only arachnologists "count the beauties" of spiders. It would undoubtedly be a quibble to point out that spiders are not insects!

May I remind the reader again that this essay is descriptive, not judicial? Wordsworth is right in maintaining that many of Pope's images are "false" from the naturalistic point of view, but I should be willing to argue that they are appropriate for the kind of poetry Pope was writing. In the metaphor just discussed, a general idea of insect-ness is what Pope wants, and he can produce it better by eclecticism than by sharp individuation.

fancy were creative; and they wished to make imagination not merely creative but a power for apprehending truth. It is a pity that neither of them was ever very clear on the subject. Perhaps the problem is too profound to allow of perfectly clear statement, but it is possible to be a lot clearer than either of them ever was.[20] In particular, I should advise the reader to note carefully what Wordsworth says about fancy in the Preface of 1815, but not to bother with what is said there about the imagination, for he will only find it confusing. Here is the passage about fancy:

"The law under which the processes of Fancy are carried on is as capricious as the accidents of things, and the effects are surprising, playful, ludicrous, amusing, tender, or pathetic, as the objects happen to be appositely produced or fortunately combined. Fancy depends upon the rapidity and profusion with which she scatters her thoughts and images; trusting that their number, and the felicity with which they are linked together, will make amends for the want of individual value: or she prides herself upon the curious subtilty and the successful elaboration with which she can detect their lurking affinities. If she can win you over to her purpose, and impart to you her feelings, she cares not how unstable or transitory may be her influence, knowing that it will not be out of her power to resume it upon an apt occasion. But the Imagination is conscious of an indestructible dominion;—the Soul may fall away from it, not being able to sustain its grandeur; but, if once felt and acknowledged, by no act of any other faculty of the mind can it be relaxed, impaired, or diminished.—Fancy is given to quicken and to beguile the temporal part of our nature, Imagination to incite and to support the eternal."

Fancy deals with images that are fixed, detailed, and sharply defined; its effects are "surprising, playful, ludicrous, amusing,

[20] The clearest and most useful treatment of the matter is by D. G. James, in *Scepticism and Poetry*, London, 1937, a book to which I am deeply indebted.

tender, or pathetic." Furthermore (and most important), these effects are transitory because the deep relationships of things will not permit a serious, steady contemplation of them in that mode. Dorothy's charming image of the tired daffodils resting their heads on the stones was for Wordsworth an image of fancy; her image of the daffodils as a busy crowd expressing social glee, an image of the imagination. He did not disparage poetry of the fancy, but he considered it inferior to poetry of the imagination. He thought that an unfortunately large portion of metaphysical poetry was fanciful rather than imaginative, because of the definiteness and fixity of its images; and he would probably have passed the same judgment on modern poetry. Imagination, in his opinion, gets at relationships that are true at the deepest level of experience. He was, in short, a religious poet; and nothing for him was deeply imaginative unless it attained (I fall back on Hartley's terminology again) to theopathy and the moral sense. And since Wordsworth was a mystic, subject to occasional mystic rapture, he felt that the deepest truth was not attained until the light of sense went out. He always connected deeply imaginative effects with the sense of infinity. So long as you can see sharply, clearly, with the kind and degree of detail that accompanies common perception, he might say, you should suspect that you are either engaged in merely practical activity or are resting in the mode of fancy. You will know that you are dealing with imagination when the edges of things begin to waver and fade out. In two brief texts he sums up the whole business far more satisfactorily than in the entire Preface devoted to the subject. The first is in the Sixth Book of *The Prelude* (he is speaking specifically of the imagination):

> in such strength
> Of usurpation, when the light of sense
> Goes out, but with a flash that has revealed
> The invisible world, doth greatness make abode,

THE EYE AND THE OBJECT

> There harbours; whether we be young or old,
> Our destiny, our being's heart and home,
> Is with infinitude, and only there;
> With hope it is, hope that can never die,
> Effort, and expectation, and desire,
> And something evermore about to be.[21]

The second occurs in a letter to Walter Savage Landor, January 21, 1824. Landor has said that he is disgusted with all books that treat of religion. Wordsworth replies that it is perhaps a bad sign in himself, but he has little relish for any other kind. "Even in poetry it is the imaginative only *viz.*, that which is conversant [with], or turns upon infinity, that powerfully affects me—perhaps I ought to explain: I mean to say that, unless in those passages where things are lost in each other, and limits vanish, and aspirations are raised, I read with something too much like indifference."[22]

It is not difficult by Wordsworth's own standards to establish the right of *I wandered lonely* to be considered an imaginative poem. The impression that the daffodils are joyous is not for him what Ruskin called pathetic fallacy. Under steady, prolonged, and serious contemplation daffodils can remain for him a symbol of joy because it is his faith (literally—no figure of speech) that every flower enjoys the air it breathes.[23] Again, *I wandered lonely* is imaginative because the impression of joy deepens into *social* joy: since the daffodils stand for men in society, the poem attains to sympathy on Hartley's ladder. But Wordsworth was not willing to rank the poem as an example of the higher exercise of the imagination, because it lacks the fade-out. In it things only just begin to be lost in each other, and limits to vanish, and aspirations to be raised.

[21] Text of 1850, vi, 599-608.
[22] *The Letters of William and Dorothy Wordsworth: The Later Years*, ed. by E. de Selincourt, 3 vols., Oxford, 1939, i, 134-5.
[23] *Lines Written in Early Spring*.

He was quite aware of the fact that *I wandered lonely* is a very simple poem.

The Solitary Reaper has the degree of complexity necessary for full illustration of Wordsworth's theory.[24] The Highland Lass is *single*, is *solitary*, is *alone*, and her song is *melancholy*. I said that the situation of *I wandered lonely* was promising, but here is what is for Wordsworth the optimum situation: solitude, in the single human figure against the landscape with more than a hint of visionary dreariness in it; society, its affections and passions presented not directly but felt in the distanced, muted, managed form of song. Actual men in crowds are to him an unmanageable sight;[25] a crowd of daffodils can stand for humanity if no more is called for than a gush of social joy; but this symbol of the singing reaper will express the whole solemn mystery of human existence. The limits begin to vanish in the first stanza with the figure of the sound overflowing the rim of the vale.

The mystery of human existence: that is the first meaning of the bird metaphors of the second stanza. The song can stand for mystery because it is itself mysterious. Like the song of the nightingale and the song of the cuckoo, it is in a foreign tongue. It is one of those Gaelic occupational chants that go on and on like the drone of a bagpipe ("the Maiden sang As if her song could have no ending"):[26] the poet feels it to be melancholy from its tone and rhythm, though he cannot under-

[24] The poem is printed at the end of this essay. Like *I wandered lonely*, the lines had a verbalized source, the then unpublished *Tour in Scotland* by Wordsworth's agriculturist friend Thomas Wilkinson. Dorothy's *Recollections of a Tour Made in Scotland* seems to say that though she and William saw *companies* of reapers, they knew of the *solitary* reaper only from Wilkinson's account. *Journals of Dorothy Wordsworth*, I, 380. After appearing among "Poems of the Imagination" in the editions of 1815 and 1820, the poem was put back into "Memorials of a Tour in Scotland, 1803," the classification which it had in the first place (1807). It was written in November 1805, just about two years after the actual tour.

[25] *The Prelude* (1850), VII, 732.

[26] The literal precision of these lines was pointed out to me by Professor David Daiches.

stand the words. But he is also at work in other ways to make limits vanish: he pushes his boundaries out in space from Arabia to St. Kilda. And the third stanza, besides reinforcing "melancholy" by the more explicit "old, unhappy, far-off things, And battles long ago," extends the boundaries in time: from "long ago" to "to-day," a plane of extension cutting across the plane of space. Again, we have the extension in human experience: from the unnatural sorrows of battles to the natural pain of everyday life.[27] It is by devices such as these that Wordsworth transfigures the matter of common perception.

It would be perverse to attempt to identify the basic ideas of Wordsworth and Blake on the imagination. Blake by his "double vision" no doubt meant much the same thing as Wordsworth with his two ways of looking steadily at objects. Wordsworth might well have joined Blake's prayer to be kept from single vision and Newton's sleep.[28] But Wordsworth believed that poetry must hold firm to the vision of the outward eye, and Blake, I think, wanted to relinquish the control of common perception altogether. "I assert for My Self that I do not behold the outward Creation & that to me it is hindrance & not Action; it is as the dirt upon my feet, No part of Me. . . . I question not my Corporeal or Vegetative Eye any more than I would Question a Window concerning a Sight. I look thro' it & not with it."[29] Still, detached from Blake's private interpre-

[27] This borrows a good deal from W. K. Wimsatt, "The Structure of the 'Concrete Universal' in Literature," *PMLA*, Vol. LXII, No. 1 (March 1947), 274-5.

[28] Letter to Thomas Butts, November 22, 1802. *Poetry and Prose of William Blake* (Nonesuch one-volume), ed. by Geoffrey Keynes, third edition, London, 1932, 1066-8.

[29] *Ibid.*, 844 (end of "A Vision of the Last Judgment"). See Blake's note written in Wordsworth's *Poems*, 1815: "Natural Objects always did & now do weaken, deaden & obliterate Imagination in Me. Wordsworth must know that what he Writes Valuable is Not to be found in Nature" (*Ibid.*, 1024-5); see also Crabb Robinson's record of Blake's remark, "Everything is *Atheism* which assumes the reality of the Natural & Unspiritual world," and of Blake's repeated charge that Wordsworth was an atheist because he loved Nature. *Blake, Coleridge, Words-*

FREDERICK A. POTTLE

tations, his lines state very well what Wordsworth proposed:

> To see a World in a Grain of Sand
> And a Heaven in a Wild Flower,
> Hold Infinity in the palm of your hand
> And Eternity in an hour.

---

worth, Lamb, etc., being Selections from the Remains of Henry Crabb Robinson, ed. by Edith J. Morley, London, 1922, 6, 10, 11, 15, 23.

I WANDERED LONELY AS A CLOUD

I wandered lonely as a cloud
That floats on high o'er vales and hills,
When all at once I saw a crowd,
A host, of golden daffodils;
Beside the lake, beneath the trees,
Fluttering and dancing in the breeze.

Continuous as the stars that shine
And twinkle on the milky way,
They stretched in never-ending line
Along the margin of a bay:
Ten thousand saw I at a glance,
Tossing their heads in sprightly dance.

The waves beside them danced; but they
Out-did the sparkling waves in glee:
A poet could not but be gay,
In such a jocund company:
I gazed—and gazed—but little thought
What wealth the show to me had brought:

For oft, when on my couch I lie
In vacant or in pensive mood,
They flash upon that inward eye
Which is the bliss of solitude;
And then my heart with pleasure fills,
And dances with the daffodils.

Behold her, single in the field,
Yon solitary Highland Lass!
Reaping and singing by herself;
Stop here, or gently pass!
Alone she cuts and binds the grain,
And sings a melancholy strain;
O listen! for the Vale profound
Is overflowing with the sound.

No Nightingale did ever chaunt
More welcome notes to weary bands
Of travellers in some shady haunt,
Among Arabian sands:
A voice so thrilling ne'er was heard
In spring-time from the Cuckoo-bird,
Breaking the silence of the seas
Among the farthest Hebrides.

Will no one tell me what she sings?—
Perhaps the plaintive numbers flow
For old, unhappy, far-off things,
And battles long ago:
Or is it some more humble lay,
Familiar matter of to-day?
Some natural sorrow, loss, or pain,
That has been, and may be again?

Whate'er the theme, the Maiden sang
As if her song could have no ending;
I saw her singing at her work,
And o'er the sickle bending:—
I listened, motionless and still;
And, as I mounted up the hill,
The music in my heart I bore,
Long after it was heard no more.

WORDSWORTH
THROUGH COLERIDGE'S EYES

BY EARL LESLIE GRIGGS

THE general theme of this symposium being "Wordsworth After One Hundred Years," it will not be amiss, perhaps, to consider and weigh Samuel Taylor Coleridge's estimate of a fellow poet. Coleridge, more than any other literary figure of his day, was on intimate terms with Wordsworth during the most productive years of the elder poet's career and left behind in his letters a passing record of his impressions, both personal and critical, and in his *Biographia Literaria* the first important critique of Wordsworth's theory and practice. Since the lives of these two poets are so inextricably interwoven, however, any attempt to discover Coleridge's interpretation of Wordsworth must inevitably involve to some degree Wordsworth's evaluation of Coleridge.

At the onset we must be on our guard, first, against the exaggerations which quite naturally found expression in Coleridge's early letters—for no man was more prone to enthusiastic encomia than he—and second, against Coleridge's sense of an esprit de corps among literary men which led him to spare the feelings of contemporary writers in public. Consider, for example, the jesting though scathing comments on Scott's *Lady of the Lake* in a letter to Wordsworth,[1] alongside the masterly defense of Sir Walter against the charge of plagiarism from *Christabel*, in a letter to a less intimate admirer,[2] or his statement that some of Southey's verses "bore the same relation to metre that dumb bells do to music—both being for exercise and pretty severe too,"[3] in the light of his praise of

[1] *Unpublished Letters of Samuel Taylor Coleridge*, ed. by E. L. Griggs, 2 vols., London, 1932, II, 37-42.
[2] *Ibid.*, 61-7.
[3] *Coleridge Fille*, by E. L. Griggs, London, 1940, 194.

45

Southey in the *Biographia Literaria*. We must be prepared, then, for overstatement in Coleridge's early letters, and we must recognize that the criticism of Wordsworth in the *Biographia Literaria* was written not from a desire to exhibit his weaknesses but, as Coleridge says, to "secure an intelligent admiration" of his poems.

The main outlines of the Wordsworth-Coleridge association are common knowledge, but some consideration of their personal relations will be necessary for this study. The two men met in Bristol, presumably late in 1795, but it was not until the spring of 1797 that their intimacy ripened. Nearly fifty years later Wordsworth remembered how Coleridge, coming to pay a visit to him and his sister at Racedown in Dorsetshire, "did not keep to the high road, but leaped over a gate and bounded down a pathless field."[4] Open-hearted and frank, buoyant and boyish, voluble and learned, Coleridge broke through Wordsworth's habitual reserve and won in an instant the affection and respect of both Wordsworth and Dorothy.

"His conversation," Dorothy wrote at this time, "teems with soul, mind, and spirit. Then he is so benevolent, so good tempered and cheerful, and, like William, interests himself so much about every little trifle. At first I thought him very plain, that is, for about three minutes: he is pale and thin, has a wide mouth, thick lips, and not very good teeth, longish loose-growing half-curling rough black hair. But if you hear him speak for five minutes you think no more of them. His eye is large and full, not dark but grey; such an eye as would receive from a heavy soul the dullest expression; but it speaks every emotion of his animated mind. . . .

"The first thing that was read after he came was William's new poem *The Ruined Cottage* with which he was much delighted; and after tea he repeated to us two acts and a half of

[4] *The Letters of William and Dorothy Wordsworth: The Later Years,* ed. by E. de Selincourt, 3 vols., Oxford, 1939, III, 1263.

his tragedy *Osorio*. The next morning William read his tragedy *The Borderers*."[5]

Thus was launched one of the most famous of literary friendships.

Coleridge, then in his twenty-fifth year, had made something of a reputation for himself by the publication of his poems and his periodical, *The Watchman*, while Wordsworth, despite the appearance of two small volumes of poetry, was as yet unheralded; but Coleridge instinctively recognized the genius of Wordsworth and began a hero-worship which was to last for many years. "Wordsworth admires my Tragedy," he wrote while still at Racedown to his publisher, Joseph Cottle, "which gives me great hopes. . . . I speak with heartfelt sincerity & (I think) unblinded judgement, when I tell you, that I feel myself a *little man by his* side; & yet do not think myself the less man, than I formerly thought myself.—His Drama is absolutely wonderful. You know, I do not commonly speak in such abrupt & unmingled phrases—& therefore will the more readily believe me.—There are in the piece those *profound* touches of the human heart, which I find three or four times in 'The Robbers' of Schiller, & often in Shakespere—but in Wordsworth there are no *inequalities*. T. Poole's opinion of Wordsworth is—that he is the greatest Man, he ever knew—I coincide."[6]

Racedown being over thirty miles from his own cottage at Nether Stowey, Coleridge determined to have Wordsworth and Dorothy nearer at hand, and since they were equally anxious to foster a friendship so auspiciously begun, he soon had them settled at Alfoxden three miles away. His enthusiasm for Wordsworth fills his letters. "Wordsworth," he wrote to Robert

[5] *The Early Letters of William and Dorothy Wordsworth*: (*1787-1805*), ed. by E. de Selincourt, Oxford, 1935, 168-9.

[6] *Letters of Samuel Taylor Coleridge*, ed. by E. H. Coleridge, 2 vols., London, 1895, I, 221. My text, however, is taken from the original manuscript. In all subsequent footnotes (MS.) following the bibliographical entry indicates my use of the manuscript source.

Southey, "is a very great man, the only man to whom *at all times* and *in all modes of excellence* I feel myself inferior";[7] and to Cottle he exclaimed: "The Giant Wordsworth—God love him!—even when I speak in the terms of admiration due to his intellect, I fear lest tho[se] terms should keep out of sight the amiableness of his manners—he has written near 1200 lines of a blank verse, superior, I hesitate not to aver, to any thing in our language which any way resembles it."[8]

The following unpublished letter written in couplets will show the easy familiarity existing between the two men. Coleridge asks an opinion concerning his poem, *The Nightingale*:

> In stale blank verse a subject stale
> I send *per post* my *Nightingale*;
> And like an honest bard, dear Wordsworth,
> You'll tell me what you think, my Bird's worth.
> My own opinion's briefly this—
> His *bill* he opens not amiss;
> And when he has sung a stave or so,
> His breast, & some small space below,
> So throbs & swells, that you might swear
> No vulgar music's working there.
> So far, so good; but then, 'od rot him!
> There's something falls off at his bottom.
> Yet, sure, no wonder it should breed,
> That my Bird's Tail's a tail indeed
> And makes it's own inglorious harmony
> Æolio crepitû, non carmine.

Almost concurrently with his association with Coleridge, Wordsworth's genius burst into full bloom, and under the benign influence of one who read only to praise he wrote such superb poems as *Tintern Abbey*. Coleridge, too, suddenly and almost miraculously found himself and in one unbelievable

[7] *Ibid.*, 224.
[8] *Ibid.*, 239. (MS.) Coleridge refers to *The Recluse*. See pp. 51-3.

year not only perfected his intimate, meditative style in such conversation poems as *This Lime-tree Bower my Prison*, but suddenly emerged as the author of those poems in which the supernatural so easily harmonizes with reality. If, on the one hand, Coleridge roused Wordsworth to a realization of his capacities, Wordsworth, for his part, seems to have unleashed in Coleridge a veritable flood of creative productivity.

In these days of early intimacy the two poets were in almost daily communion. Much talk there was of poetry and poetic expression; much experimentation and even efforts at collaboration took place; until out of that caldron of impassioned conversation came a slim anonymous volume entitled *Lyrical Ballads*. In it were printed four poems by Coleridge and nineteen by Wordsworth. Although it contained such diverse poems as *Tintern Abbey* and *We are Seven*, with its direct simplicity of expression, and *The Rime of the Ancyent Marinere*, which in its early form was embellished with archaic words and spellings, no hint of dual authorship was indicated.

The Advertisement prefixed to the first edition of *Lyrical Ballads* modestly asserts: "The majority of the following poems are to be considered as experiments. They were written chiefly with a view to ascertain how far the language of conversation in the middle and lower classes of society is adapted to the purposes of poetic pleasure." While there is a passing reference to the "Ancyent Marinere" as "professedly written in imitation of the *style*, as well as of the spirit of the elder poets," it is evident that the Advertisement, brief as it is, emphasizes Wordsworth's and not Coleridge's poems, and it was not until the appearance of the *Biographia Literaria* in 1817 that an adequate explanation of the contrast between the aims of the authors was revealed. Writing in that work, Coleridge says that out of the early conversations between himself and Wordsworth the plan of the *Lyrical Ballads* originated. It was agreed, he continues:

". . . that my endeavours should be directed to persons and

characters supernatural, or at least romantic. . . . Mr. Wordsworth, on the other hand, was to propose to himself as his
object, to give the charm of novelty to things of every day, and
to excite a feeling analogous to the supernatural, by awakening the mind's attention from the lethargy of custom, and
directing it to the loveliness and the wonders of the world
before us. . . . With this view I wrote 'The Ancient Mariner,'
and was preparing among other poems, . . . the 'Christabel.'
. . . But Mr. Wordsworth's industry had proved so much more
successful, and the number of his poems so much greater, that
my compositions, instead of forming a balance, appeared rather
an interpolation of heterogeneous matter. Mr. Wordsworth
added two or three poems written in his own character. . . .
In this form the 'Lyrical Ballads' were published; and were
presented by him, as an *experiment.*"[9]

Throughout these discussions on the nature of poetry,
Wordsworth had fixed his attention on subjects drawn from
everyday life and presented in unadorned language, and, far
from agreeing with Coleridge's choice of supernatural themes,
he composed *Peter Bell,* in what Raleigh calls "a barely con-
cealed competitive intent."[10] In a dedicatory letter published
with the poem in 1819, Wordsworth says he wished to prove
that "the Imagination not only does not require for its exercise
the intervention of supernatural agency, but . . . may be called
forth as imperiously . . . by incidents within the compass of
poetic probability, in the humblest departments of daily life."
The poem is, of course, no rival of *The Ancient Mariner,* but its
composition shows that Wordsworth tried to create "a feeling
analogous to the supernatural" from natural causes. That he
did not recognize how superbly Coleridge succeeded in hold-
ing his readers spellbound by the use of supernatural agency
is evidence of his own limitations.

[9] *Biographia Literaria,* ed. by J. Shawcross, 2 vols., London, 1907, II,
5-6.
[10] *Wordsworth,* by Walter Raleigh, London, 1921, 74.

It would be erroneous to assume that discussions between Wordsworth and Coleridge were limited to matters concerning *Lyrical Ballads*. Of great importance is the inception of Wordsworth's philosophical poem, *The Recluse*. As early as March 1798, Wordsworth wrote to a friend that he had completed 1,300 lines "of a poem in which I contrive to convey most of the knowledge of which I am possessed. My object is to give pictures of Nature, Man, and Society. Indeed I know not any thing which will not come within the scope of my plan."[11]

Nowhere in Wordsworth's letters or notes is there any clear explanation of what he intended to accomplish in *The Recluse*, and it is to Coleridge rather than to Wordsworth that we must turn for a description of its magnitude, aims, and purposes. According to Coleridge, who outlined the plan for the poem in a letter written in 1815, Wordsworth was first "to have meditated the faculties of Man in the abstract . . . [and] to have laid a solid and immoveable foundation . . . by removing the sandy Sophisms of Locke, and the Mechanic Dogmatists." Secondly, he was to "take the Human Race in the concrete," and exploding the idea of "Man's having progressed from an Ouran Outang state" to affirm "a Fall in some sense, as a fact." Thirdly, after treating of "Fallen men . . . in the different ages of the World," he was to point out "a manifest Scheme of Redemption from the Slavery, of Reconciliation from this Enmity with Nature." Finally, he was "to conclude by a grand didactic swell on the necessary identity of a true Philosophy with true Religion."[12] Thus Coleridge seems to have been responsible for the philosophical depth of the design for *The Recluse*.

[11] *The Early Letters*, 188.
[12] *Letters of Coleridge*, II, 648-9. (MS.) On July 21, 1832, Coleridge again described the design of *The Recluse*: "The plan laid out, and, I believe, partly suggested by me, was, that Wordsworth should assume the station of a man in mental repose, one whose principles were made up, and so prepared to deliver upon authority a system of philosophy. He was to treat man as man,—a subject of eye, ear, touch, and taste, in contact with external nature, and informing the senses from the mind, and

The Recluse was never completed, for by the winter of 1798-1799, Wordsworth turned aside to an autobiographical poem, which he considered both as a testing ground for his powers and as an introduction to the more ambitious task. *The Prelude,* as this poem is now called, was completed by 1805, but was neither published nor given its present title until after his death. Certainly he found it a more congenial task than *The Recluse,* for his mind naturally turned in upon itself; and it was probably Coleridge's bewitching conversation which led him to an overconfidence in his ability to produce the larger philosophical poem. In 1814 he published *The Excursion* as the second part of *The Recluse* but it obviously does not carry out the original plan. In the preface to *The Excursion* Wordsworth printed a hundred odd lines from the conclusion to the first book of *The Recluse,* and later he pathetically remarked that any remaining portions of it had been incorporated into his other poems. *The Recluse,* then, though its non-fulfillment continued to haunt Wordsworth until his death, was only an unrealized dream.[13]

One can easily imagine how Coleridge, whose mind, he himself said, "is comprehensive in it's conceptions and wastes itself in the contemplations of the many things which it might do,"[14] embraced the scheme for *The Recluse.* Convinced from the

---

not compounding a mind out of the senses; then he was to describe the pastoral and other states of society, assuming something of the Juvenalian spirit as he approached the high civilization of cities and towns, and opening a melancholy picture of the present state of degeneracy and vice; thence he was to infer and reveal the proof of, and ncessity for, the whole state of man and society being subject to, and illustrative of, a redemptive process in operation, showing how this idea reconciled all the anomalies, and promised future glory and restoration. Something of this sort was, I think, agreed on. It is, in substance, what I have been all my life doing in my system of philosophy." *Specimens of the Table Talk of . . . Coleridge,* 2 vols., London, 1835, ii, 70-1.

[13] For the collected fragments of *The Recluse,* see *The Poetical Works of William Wordsworth,* ed. by E. de Selincourt and Helen Darbishire, 5 vols., Oxford, 1940-49, v, 313-62.

[14] *Letters of Coleridge,* i, 270. (MS.)

beginning of their association that Wordsworth possessed the requisite poetic and philosophic power—indeed, he later declared that Wordsworth was "a great Poet by inspirations, & in the Moments of revelation, but . . . a thinking feeling Philosopher habitually—"[15] Coleridge was impatient of anything likely to interfere with the composition of this philosophical work. In the summer of 1799 we find him not only urging Wordsworth to take up *The Recluse* but also dropping a hint which contains the seed of more than one book of *The Excursion*. "My dear friend," Coleridge wrote: "I do entreat you go on with 'The Recluse'; and I wish you would write a poem, in blank verse, addressed to those, who, in consequence of the complete failure of the French Revolution, have thrown up all hopes of the amelioration of mankind, and are sinking into an almost epicurean selfishness, disguising the same under the soft titles of domestic attachment and contempt for visionary *philosophes*. It would do great good, and might form a part of 'The Recluse,' for in my present mood I am wholly against the publication of any small poems."[16]

Coleridge reiterated his entreaties a few weeks later. Wordsworth seems to have communicated to Coleridge his plan to produce a separate poem addressed to him, an indication that the framework of *The Prelude* was taking shape in his mind; and Coleridge, apparently not yet realizing the scope of that poem, burst forth: "I long to see what you have been doing. O let it be the tail-piece of 'The Recluse!' for of nothing but 'The Recluse' can I hear patiently. That it is to be addressed to me makes me more desirous that it should not be a poem of itself. To be addressed, as a beloved man, by a thinker, at the close of such a poem as 'The Recluse,' . . . is the only event, I believe, capable of inciting in me an hour's vanity—. . ."[17]

[15] *Unpublished Letters*, I, 266. (MS.)
[16] *Memoirs of William Wordsworth*, by Christopher Wordsworth, 2 vols., London, 1851, I, 159.
[17] *Ibid.*

Before proceeding with the intellectual association between the two men, however, we must revert briefly to their personal lives. After their golden year together, they set sail for Germany. There their paths and their interests diverged, Wordsworth spending his time in poetic composition and Coleridge in mastering the German language and the outlines of German thought. On his return in May 1799, Wordsworth, after visiting for several months with the Hutchinsons at Sockburn in Durham County, settled late in December with Dorothy in Dove Cottage, Grasmere. Yet he had been "affected to tears" at the thought of not having Coleridge near him, and as Dorothy said, they hoped to "decoy" him to the north. In the meantime, Coleridge, who did not return from Germany until July, deplored his separation from Wordsworth and in October hastened to join him at Sockburn. While there Coleridge met not only Mary Hutchinson, who was to become Wordsworth's wife in 1802, but her sister Sara, with whom he fell hopelessly in love. The details of that frustrated affair, which disrupted the hitherto amicable relations with Mrs. Coleridge and cast a shadow over the next decade of his life, need not detain us here; suffice it to say that his love for Sara Hutchinson drew him even more closely to the Wordsworth circle.

From Sockburn, Wordsworth took Coleridge on a tour of the Lake Country; and though Coleridge returned to London in November 1799, by April he had come north again, "on a visit to his god Wordsworth," as Lamb said.[18] At this time he and the Wordsworths found Greta Hall, Keswick, thirteen miles from Grasmere, and in July he settled there with his wife and child. His desire, as well as that of the Wordsworths, had been achieved; but the move was against the wishes of Mrs. Coleridge, who had little affection for them, and in the face of strong opposition from his benefactors, the Wedgwoods, and other devoted friends.

[18] *The Letters of Charles Lamb*, ed. by E. V. Lucas, 3 vols., London, 1935, I, 179.

"You charge me with prostration in regard to Wordsworth," he wrote in self-defense to Poole: "Have I affirmed anything miraculous of W.? Is it impossible that a greater poet than any since Milton may appear in our days? . . . Future greatness! Is it not an awful thing, my dearest Poole? What if you had known Milton at the age of thirty, and believed all you now know of him?—What if you should meet in the letters of any then living man, expressions concerning the young Milton *totidem verbis* the same as mine of Wordsworth, would it . . . not be an assurance to you that your admiration of the *Paradise Lost* was no superstition, . . . but that the *Man* was even so, that the greatness was incarnate and personal? Wherein blame I you, my best friend? Only in being borne down by other men's rash opinions concerning W. You yourself, for yourself, judged wisely."[19]

Elsewhere he remarked to Poole that "the Society of so great a Being is of priceless Value," and went on to accept Wordsworth's determination to live in the Lake Country: "He will never quit the North of England—his habits are more assimilated with the Inhabitants there—there he and his Sister are exceedingly beloved, enthusiastically. Such difference do small Sympathies make—such as Voice, Pronunciation, etc—for from what other Cause can I account for it—[20] Certainly, no one, neither you, or the Wedgwoods, altho you far more than any one else, ever entered into the feeling due to a man like Wordsworth—of whom I do not hesitate in saying, that since Milton no man has *manifested* himself equal to him."[21]

Coleridge felt that he was necessary to Wordsworth, whose "genius is most *apparent* in poetry—and rarely, except to me in tete a tete, breaks forth in conversational eloquence."[22] Even more pointedly he wrote to Poole: "My many weaknesses are

[19] *Thomas Poole and His Friends,* by Mrs. Henry Sandford, 2 vols., London, 1888, II, 8.
[20] From an unpublished portion of a letter to Thomas Poole.
[21] Mrs. Henry Sandford, *op. cit.,* II, 7. (MS.)
[22] *Letters of Coleridge,* I, 246. (MS.)

of some advantage to me; they unite me more with the great mass of my fellow-beings—but dear Wordsworth appears to me to have hurtfully segregated and isolated his Being. Doubtless, his delights are more deep and sublime; but he has likewise more hours, that prey on his flesh and blood."[23]

/ Despite the accuracy of these analyses, Coleridge did not quite truly assess the relationship between himself and Wordsworth. Having profited so greatly from his early association and approving everything Wordsworth said and did, he seems to have supposed that his affection and sympathy were reciprocated. His affection was, I believe, fully returned; but Wordsworth soon became too self-centered wholly to sympathize with him. He could love Coleridge and pity him, but he could not give, as Coleridge did, that warm encouragement born of idolatry. Wordsworth was the stronger man, as Coleridge was the more magnetic, and in the long run the gain was his, not Coleridge's.[24]

Since the summer of 1799, Wordsworth had been brooding over the fate of Lyrical Ballads—"William's poems," as Dorothy always referred to them—and planning a second edition. Noting that Southey in the Critical Review[25] had selected The Ancient Mariner for special scorn and believing that that poem

[23] Ibid., 297. (MS.)

[24] Ten years later, after he and Wordsworth had quarrelled, Coleridge came to realize how one-sided their friendship had been. While there is an element of self-pity in the following statement, the analysis, nevertheless, seems correct: "The events of the last year [1810], and emphatically of the last month [October], have now forced me to perceive—no one on earth has ever LOVED me. Doubtless, the fault must have been partly, perhaps chiefly in myself. The want of reliability in little things, the infliction of little pains, the trifling with hope, in short, all that render the idea of any person recall more pain than pleasures— these would account for the loss of friendship. But that I never possessed it in reality, but only that semblance of friendship, the being pleased with my admiration and attachment—this I believe owing in part to my voluntary self-humiliation, my habitual abasement of myself and talents in comparison with the merits of my friend. For alas! even in love and friendship we gain only what we arrogate." T. M. Raysor, "Coleridge and 'Asra,' " Studies in Philology, Vol. xxvi, No. 3 (July 1929), 322-3.

[25] The Critical Review, Vol. xxiv, October 1798.

had aroused general antagonism to the whole volume, as early as June 1799 he questioned the advisability of including it in a new edition. "From what I can gather," he wrote to Cottle, "it seems that The Ancyent Marinere has upon the whole been an injury to the volume, I mean that the old words and the strangeness of it have deterred readers from going on. If the volume should come to a second edition I would put in its place some little things which would be more likely to suit the common taste."[26]

Nevertheless, reading a little later a favorable review in the *British Critic*,[27] where the volume was attributed to Coleridge, and hearing that several persons had made the same ascription, he begged Coleridge to "take no pains to contradict the story that the L.B. are entirely yours. Such a rumour is the best thing that can befall them."[28] The inescapable conclusion is that Wordsworth was at this time interested solely in the reception of the first edition of *Lyrical Ballads*. He not only recovered the copyright for himself but adopted a patronizing attitude towards *The Ancient Mariner*.

Coleridge accepted Wordsworth's animadversions and with characteristic disregard for his own production "desired that his Jonah should be thrown overboard"; instead, however, he removed the archaisms in accordance with Wordsworth's wishes and extensively revised his poem for the new edition of *Lyrical Ballads* to be published in two volumes under Wordsworth's name.[29] He also gave the poem the subtitle, "A Poet's Reverie," possibly to overcome Wordsworth's objections to its "strangeness" and to prevent moral judgment of its story in terms of reality. Charles Lamb was quick to notice the incongruity of the new title: "What new idea is gained by this Title, but one subversive of all credit, which the tale

[26] *The Early Letters*, 226-7.
[27] *The British Critic*, Vol. xiv, October 1799.
[28] *The Early Letters*, 242.
[29] *Cf.* B. R. McElderry, "Coleridge's Revision of 'The Ancient Mariner,'" *Studies in Philology*, Vol. xxix, No. 1 (January 1932), 68-94.

should force upon us, of its truth?"[30] Yet Wordsworth, not content with Coleridge's revisions, publicly disparaged the poem by printing a note in *Lyrical Ballads* to justify its inclusion. Without any allusion to the revisions, Wordsworth begins: "I cannot refuse myself the gratification of informing such Readers as may have been pleased with this Poem . . . that they owe their pleasure in some sort to me; as the Author was himself very desirous that it should be suppressed. This wish had arisen from a consciousness of the defects of the Poem, and from a knowledge that many persons had been much displeased with it. The Poem of my Friend has indeed great defects."

He then proceeds to enumerate the faults: "The principal person has no distinct character, either in his profession of Mariner, or as a human being who having been long under the controul of supernatural impressions might be supposed himself to partake of something supernatural: . . . he does not act, but is continually acted upon: . . . the events having no necessary connection do not produce each other; and . . . the imagery is somewhat too laboriously accumulated."[31] Although Wordsworth concludes his note with qualified praise, its inclusion in *Lyrical Ballads* was ungenerous and even unfriendly, and unmistakably reveals his inability to appreciate Coleridge's supernatural masterpiece.

At first it was planned to include *Christabel* in the enlarged edition of *Lyrical Ballads;* but Coleridge, though he succeeded in adding Part II in a burst of creative activity, could not bring his poem to completion. The following letter from Coleridge to Humphry Davy, however, shows that other reasons than its fragmentary nature explain its exclusion:

"The Christabel was running up to 1300 lines—[a palpable exaggeration!] and was so much admired by Wordsworth,

[30] *The Letters of Charles Lamb*, i, 240.
[31] *The Road to Xanadu*, by J. L. Lowes, Boston, 1927, 520. This note was omitted in the 1802 and 1805 editions of *Lyrical Ballads*.

that he thought it indelicate to print two Volumes with his name in which so much of another man's was included—& which was of more consequence—the poem was in direct opposition to the very purpose for which the Lyrical Ballads were published—viz—an experiment to see how far those passions, which alone give any value to extraordinary Incidents, were capable of interesting, in & for themselves, in the incidents of common Life. . . . I assure you, I think very differently of *Christabel*—I would rather have written Ruth . . . than a million such poems; but why do I calumniate my own spirit by saying, *I* would rather—God knows—it is as delightful to me that they *are* written."[32]

The rejection of *Christabel* and Wordsworth's condescending attitude toward *The Ancient Mariner* probably reacted more unfavorably upon Coleridge's creative power than has hitherto been suspected. To a friend he wrote in September 1800: "I abandon Poetry altogether—I leave the higher & deeper Kind, to Wordsworth, the delightful, popular & simply dignified to Southey; & reserve for myself the honorable attempt to make others feel and understand their writings, as they deserve to be felt and understood."[33]

Six months later he declared to Godwin: "The Poet is dead in me—My imagination (or rather the Somewhat that had been imaginative) lies, like a Cold Snuff on the circular Rim of a Brass Candle-stick, without even a stink of Tallow to remind you, that it was once cloathed and mitred with Flame. That is past by!—I was once a Volume of Gold Leaf, rising and riding on every breath of Fancy—but I have beaten myself back into weight and density, and now I sink in quicksilver. . . . If I die, and the Booksellers will give you any thing for my Life, be sure to say—'Wordsworth descended on him, like the Γνωθι σεαυτον from Heaven; by shewing to him what true Poetry

[32] *Letters of Coleridge*, I, 337. (MS.)
[33] From an unpublished manuscript.

was, he made him know, that he himself was no Poet.' "[34] Perhaps Coleridge was convinced that his poetry was of little consequence; certainly, he was more interested in Wordsworth's reputation than his own.

Wordsworth well understood the contradictions of Coleridge's personality, and he recorded his impressions in a poem entitled *A Character*. Nor was Coleridge displeased with the poem. "As an *Author*," he wrote to Godwin: ". . . I have neither Vanity nor Ambition—I think meanly of all, that I have done; and if ever I hope proudly of my future Self, this Hot Fit is uniformly followed and punished by Languor, and Despondency—or rather, by lazy and unhoping indifference.—In the 2nd Volume of Wordsworth's Lyrical Ballads you will find certain *parts,* and superficies of me sketched truly under the title—'A character in the antithetical manner.' "[35] Turning to Wordsworth's poem, we can only agree:

I marvel how Nature could ever find space
For so many strange contrasts in one human face:
There's thought and no thought, and there's paleness and
  bloom
And bustle and sluggishness, pleasure and gloom.

There's weakness, and strength both redundant and vain;
Such strength as, if ever affliction and pain
Could pierce through a temper that's soft to disease,
Would be rational peace—a philosopher's ease.

There's indifference, alike when he fails or succeeds,
And attention full ten times as much as there needs;
Pride where there's no envy, there's so much of joy;
And mildness, and spirit both forward and coy.

There's freedom, and sometimes a diffident stare
Of shame scarcely seeming to know that she's there,

[34] *William Godwin,* by C. Kegan Paul, 2 vols., London, 1876, II, 78-9. (MS.)
[35] From an unpublished manuscript.

There's virtue, the title it surely may claim,
Yet wants heaven knows what to be worthy the name.

This picture from nature may seem to depart,
Yet the Man would at once run away with your heart;
And I for five centuries right gladly would be
Such an odd such a kind happy creature as he.

The second edition of *Lyrical Ballads* was designed to establish the reputation of Wordsworth, who was led to add his famous Preface wherein he propounded a theory of poetry adequate, he believed, to explain his departure from the poetry of his age. Coleridge not only concurred with much of Wordsworth's theory but was responsible for certain parts of it; and he plunged into a campaign to insure the success of the *Lyrical Ballads*. He arranged to have Davy work with the printers; he wrote glowing letters of praise to his friends; and once the volumes were out, he encouraged Wordsworth to send them, along with explanatory letters, to eminent persons. If ever a man dedicated himself to another, he did so; and he was untroubled by the fact that his name was nowhere mentioned, Wordsworth merely referring to "the assistance of a friend" to account for the five poems Coleridge contributed.

With the appearance of the work in January 1801, Wordsworth had launched his poetic career. With stubborn perseverance he had charted his course and nothing could swerve him from it. Coleridge, on the contrary, was now a broken, dispirited man, rudderless and undisciplined. He did not complete his projected life of Lessing, he did not become, as Daniel Stuart wished, a regular contributor to the *Morning Post*, and *Christabel*, unfinished and unregarded, had been flung aside. For one who could "spawn plans like a herring" his achievement during these years is pathetic. Yet his failures were not entirely due to volitional paralysis. Residence in the north of England was most harmful to his health and brought on a greatly increased indulgence in opium; open discord between himself and Mrs. Coleridge and a growing sense of frustration arising out of his love for Sara Hutchinson, now often a guest at Grasmere, kept him in a state of internal turmoil; and Wordsworth's failure to appreciate his poetry and give him the encouragement he needed undermined his self-confidence. Thus it is not surprising that in April 1802 he should have penned his saddest poem, *Dejection: an Ode,* wherein he bade farewell to his "shaping spirit of Imagination."

With the publication in 1802 of the third edition of *Lyrical Ballads,* in which Wordsworth greatly expanded the Preface and added an Appendix on poetic diction, Coleridge noted that both he and Wordsworth had come to suspect the existence of a *"radical* Difference" in their opinions. Writing to William Sotheby in July 1802, Coleridge says:

"[I must] set you right with regard to my perfect coinc[idence with] his poetic Creed. It is most certain, that that [partly arose from] the heads of our mutual Conversations &c.—& th[at certain pass]ages were indeed partly taken [from notes] of mine—for it was at first intended, that the Preface should be written by me and it is likewise true, that I warmly accord with W. in his abhorrence of these poetic Licences, as they are called. . . . In my opinion every phrase, every metaphor, every personification, should have it's justifying Cause in some *passion* either of the Poet's mind, or of the Characters described by the poet—But *metre itself* implies a *passion,* i.e. a state of excitement, both in the Poet's mind, & is expected in that of the Reader—and tho' I stated this to Wordsworth, & he has in some sort stated it in his preface, yet he has [not] done justice to it, nor has he in my opinion sufficiently answered it. In my opinion, Poetry justifies, as *Poetry* independent of any other Passion, some new combinations of Language, & *commands* the omission of many others allowable in other compositions. Now Wordsworth, me saltem judice, has in his system not sufficiently admitted the former, & in his practice has too frequently sinned against the latter.—Indeed, we have had lately some little controversy on this subject."[36]

Here, indeed, is an anticipation of Coleridge's later remarks in the *Biographia Literaria.* It is perhaps significant to add that at least three times in his later years (1830, 1838, 1845) Wordsworth insisted he had written the Preface in answer to Coleridge's "urgent entreaties," statements hard to equate with his reprintings of that document.[37]

Coleridge felt so strongly the divergence of opinion between himself and Wordsworth that he projected an essay on his own theory of poetry, as well as a discussion of the merits of the poetry of his contemporaries. As was characteristic of him, this work was never written. In a letter to Southey, however, he emphasized his main objections to Wordsworth's critical statements:

"Although Wordsworth's Preface is half a child of my own brain, and arose out of conversations so frequent that, with few exceptions, we could scarcely either of us, perhaps, positively say which first started any particular thought (I am speaking of the Preface as it stood in the second volume [edi-

[36] *Letters of Coleridge,* I, 373-5. (MS.) The manuscript of this letter is torn and conjectural readings are enclosed in brackets.

[37] In a letter of 1830 Wordsworth says: "I am not a Critic—and set little value upon the art. The preface which I wrote long ago to my own Poems I was put upon to write by the urgent entreaties of a friend, and heartily regret I ever had anything to do with it; though I do not reckon the principles then advanced erroneous." Again in 1838 he wrote: "Though prevailed upon by Mr Coleridge to write the first Preface to my Poems—which tempted, or rather forced, me to add a supplement to it— and induced by my friendship for him to write the Essay upon Epitaphs, now appended to The Excursion, but first composed for The Friend, I have never felt inclined to write criticism." Finally, in 1845 he said: "Having long wished that an Edition of my Poems should be published without the Prefaces and supplement, I submit to your consideration whether that would not be well. . . . The Prefaces, etc contain many important observations upon Poetry—but they were written solely to gratify Coleridge; and, for my own part, being quite against anything of the kind, and having always been of opinion that Poetry should stand upon its own merits, I would not even attach to the Poems any explanation of the grounds of their arrangement." *The Later Years,* I, 537; II, 910; III, 1248-9.

tion?]³⁸), yet I am far from going all lengths with Wordsworth. He has written lately a number of Poems . . . the greater number of these . . . very excellent compositions, but here and there a daring humbleness of language and versification, and a strict adherence to matter of fact, even to prolixity, that startled me. His alterations, likewise, in 'Ruth' perplexed me, and I have thought and thought again, and have not had my doubts solved by Wordsworth.³⁹ . . . In the new edition of the L. Ballads there is a valuable appendix, which I am sure you must like, and in the Preface itself considerable additions; one on the dignity and nature of the office and character of a Poet, that is very grand, and of a sort of Verulamian power and majesty, but it is, in parts (and this is the fault, *me judice,* of all the latter half of that Preface), obscure beyond any necessity, and the extreme elaboration and almost constrainedness of the diction contrasted (to my feelings) somewhat harshly with the general style of the Poems, to which the Preface is an introduction."⁴⁰

Once the third edition of *Lyrical Ballads* was out of the way, Coleridge renewed his efforts to encourage Wordsworth to concentrate on his philosophical poem. He wrote to Poole in 1803:

"I rejoice . . . with a deep & true Joy, that he has at length yielded to my urgent & repeated—almost unremitting—requests & remonstrances—& will go on with the Recluse exclusively.—

³⁸ Coleridge obviously refers to the Preface in the second edition of *Lyrical Ballads.*

³⁹ See the entry for August 13, 1812, in Crabb Robinson's *Diary,* where Robinson cites Coleridge as censuring Schiller "for a sort of ventriloquism in poetry" and goes on to mention *Ruth* (still presumably quoting Coleridge): "In *Ruth,* as it stands at present, there is the same fault; Wordsworth had not originally put into the mouth of the lover many of the sentiments he now entertains, and which would better have become the poet himself." *Henry Crabb Robinson on Books and Their Writers,* ed. by Edith J. Morley, 3 vols., London, 1938, I, 107. See also Shawcross, *op. cit.,* II, 109, where Coleridge speaks of "a species of ventriloquism" in Wordsworth.

⁴⁰ *Letters of Coleridge,* I, 386-7.

A Great Work . . . necessarily comprehending his attention &
Feelings within the circle of great objects & elevated Conceptions—this is his natural Element—. . . . I have seen enough,
positively to give me feelings of hostility towards the plan of
several of the Poems in the L. Ballads: & I really consider it as
a misfortune, that Wordsworth ever deserted his former moun-
tain Track to wander in Lanes & allies. . . . He found himself
to be, or rather to be called, the Head & Founder of a *Sect* in
Poetry: & assuredly he has written—& published in the M. Post,
. . . poems written with a *sectarian* spirit, & in a sort of Bra-
vado."[41]

In the same mood he confided to his notebook:

"I am sincerely glad that he has bidden farewell to all small .
poems, and is devoting himself to his great work. . . . In those
little poems, his own corrections coming of necessity so often
. . . wore him out; difference of opinion with his best friends
irritated him, and he wrote, at times, too much with a sectarian
spirit."[42]

Coleridge's persistent entreaties are not hard to understand
when we recall that he looked to Wordsworth for "the *first*
and *only* true Phil[osophical] Poem in existence,"[43] and it is
clear that Wordsworth needed his friend's genial encouragement. As he worked on *The Prelude* and looked forward to
The Recluse, he felt uncertain and more than ever sought
those suggestions and ideas emanating from Coleridge's breadth
of vision. Coleridge, however, was so far reduced in health
by early 1804 that he left the Lake Country and determined
to try the warmer climate of Malta. While he was in London
making arrangements for his passage, he apparently wrote to
Wordsworth of his intention to send a letter containing his
notes on *The Recluse,* and Wordsworth, acutely conscious of
Coleridge's procrastinating habits, emphatically urged him to

[41] *Unpublished Letters,* I, 291-2. (MS.)
[42] *Anima Poetae,* ed. by E. H. Coleridge, London, 1895, 30.
[43] *Letters of Coleridge,* II, 648. (MS.)

do so. On March 6, 1804, he wrote: "I am very anxious to have your notes for *The Recluse*. I cannot say how much importance I attach to this; if it should please God that I survive you, I should reproach myself forever in writing the work if I had neglected to procure this help."[44] Three weeks later, on the eve of Coleridge's sailing, he was even more insistent: "I cannot help saying that I would gladly have given 3 fourths of my possessions for your letter on *The Recluse*. . . . I cannot say what a load it would be to me, should I survive you and you die without this memorial left behind. Do, for heaven's sake, put this out of the reach of accident immediately."[45]

Wordsworth was never to receive these notes, for Coleridge, dilatory as ever, delayed sending them until after his arrival in Malta. They were entrusted for transmittal to England to Major Adye, who died of the plague en route and whose papers had to be destroyed. Reporting on this loss, as well as that of other letters which were thrown overboard from various ships pursued by the French, Coleridge wrote: "My Ideas respecting your Recluse were burnt as a Plague-garment, and all my long letters to you and Sir George Beaumont sunk to the bottom of the Sea!"[46]

The Wordsworths were deeply concerned over Coleridge's breakdown in health, and there are probably more references to Coleridge in their correspondence during his absence abroad than at any other period. The letters of both Dorothy and Wordsworth are filled with anxiety and affection. They now felt that the damp climate of the Lake Country had been detrimental to Coleridge's health and they were willing to live in any place likely to prove more healthful for him. Writing to Lady Beaumont, Dorothy says: "His returning to *live* in the North of England is quite out of the question, therefore we intend to keep ourselves unfettered here, ready to move to any place where he may chuse to settle with his fam-

[44] *The Early Letters*, 368.   [45] *Ibid.*, 379-80.
[46] *Ibid.*, 508, as recorded by Dorothy in a letter to Lady Beaumont.

ily."[47] And a few months later she writes: "We now have little thought of leaving our cottage till Coleridge's return which surely will not be long, and we shall go wherever he goes."[48]

Perhaps the most significant comments concerning Coleridge's help and inspiration come from Wordsworth himself. He was bringing *The Prelude* to completion while Coleridge was absent in Malta, and in May 1805 he wrote to Sir George Beaumont that "Two books more will conclude it." He considered the poem of "alarming length"—9,000 lines—and thought it "a thing unprecedented in literary history that a man should talk so much about himself." He explained why he wrote the poem: "I began the work because I was unprepared to treat any more arduous subject, and diffident of my own powers." This is quite in contrast to Coleridge's unlimited faith in Wordsworth's ability to execute *The Recluse*. Continuing in this mood of humility, Wordsworth went on to add: "If, when the work [*The Prelude*] shall be finished, it appears to the judicious to have redundancies, they shall be lopped off, if possible; but this is very difficult to do, . . . and this defect, whenever I have suspected it or found it to exist in any writings of mine, I have always found incurable. The fault lies too deep, and is in the first conception. If you see Coleridge before I do, do not speak of this to him, as I should like to have his judgment unpreoccupied by such an apprehension."[49]

By May 1805 Wordsworth had finished *The Prelude*, but he still felt doubtful of his ability to write *The Recluse*. To Sir George Beaumont he communicated his misgivings: "I finished my poem about a fortnight ago. . . . I was dejected on many accounts; when I looked back upon the performance it seemed to have a dead weight about it, the reality so far short of the expectation; it was the first long labour that I had finished, and the doubt whether I should ever live to write *The Recluse*, and the sense which I had of this poem being so far below what I seemed capable of executing, depressed me

[47] *Ibid.*, 416.   [48] *Ibid.*, 435.   [49] *Ibid.*, 489.

much. . . . *The Recluse* . . . I hope to be able, ere long, to begin
with in earnest."[50] In August 1806, a few days before Coleridge's arrival in England, he again wrote to Beaumont:
"Within this last month I have returned to the Recluse, and
have written 700 additional lines. Should Coleridge return,
so that I might have some conversation with him upon the
subject, I should go on swimmingly."[51]

When Coleridge returned from Malta, "ill, penniless, and
worse than homeless," and determined to live apart from Mrs.
Coleridge, he did not meet the Wordsworths at once, and it
was not until October that a reunion took place at an inn in
Kendal. They were startled by his appearance and state of
mind:

"Never never did I feel such a shock as at first sight of him,"
Dorothy wrote to Catherine Clarkson: "We all felt exactly in
the same way—as if he were different from what we have expected to see; almost as much as a person of whom we have
thought much, and of whom we had formed an image in our
own minds, without having any personal knowledge of him.
. . . That he is ill I am well assured, and must sink if he does
not grow more happy. His fatness has quite changed him—it
is more like the flesh of a person in a dropsy. . . . His counte-
nance. Alas! I never saw it, as it used to be—a shadow, a gleam
there was at times, but how faint and transitory! I think however that, if he have courage to go through the . . . [separation
from Mrs. Coleridge] William's conversation and our kind
offices may soothe him, and bring on tranquillity; and then,
the only hope that remains will be in his applying himself to
some grand object connected with permanent effects."[52]

Two months after this first meeting Coleridge joined the
Wordsworths and Sara Hutchinson at Coleorton, Leicestershire.
It was at this time that Wordsworth read aloud his *Prelude*.

[50] *Ibid.*, 497.
[51] *The Letters of William and Dorothy Wordsworth: The Middle Years,*
ed. by E. de Selincourt, 2 vols., Oxford, 1937, I, 51.
[52] *Ibid.*, 68-70.

Coleridge was so carried away by its power that his own poetic genius revived, and he recorded his feelings in his lines *To William Wordsworth.* In this "Orphic song," as Coleridge called it, was positive evidence of Wordsworth's ability to produce a sustained poetic composition, and sharing none of Wordsworth's misgivings about it, Coleridge could say:

> O great Bard! . . .
> With stedfast eye I viewed thee in the choir
> Of ever-enduring men.

Coleridge never lost his admiration for this poem. Two years before his death he said: "I cannot help regretting that Wordsworth did not first publish his thirteen books on the growth of an individual mind. . . . You may judge how I felt about them by my own poem upon the occasion."[53]

The Prelude as Wordsworth read it to Coleridge was not, of course, the 1850 version to which most readers are accustomed but the 1805 text which was first published by Professor de Selincourt in 1926. We cannot consider the innumerable changes which Wordsworth made during his lifetime, but two or three observations may be noted. As the plan for *The Prelude* was shaping itself in Wordsworth's mind in the summer of 1799, he determined to address the poem to Coleridge. At that time Coleridge, as we have seen, thought of the poem as the "tail-piece" of *The Recluse,* and he continued to consider it, as Wordsworth did, as "tributary" or "introductory" to *The Recluse.* Moreover, in dedicating the poem to Coleridge, Wordsworth was consciously giving his autobiographical materials a center and direction, and it seems evident that he was heavily indebted to Coleridge for inspiration as well as for philosophical suggestions. It is worth remarking, too, that when Coleridge left for Malta, he took with him a copy of the first five books of *The Prelude* for solace during his long separation. As Wordsworth directed Dorothy and Mary in making the

[53] *Table Talk,* II, 70.

transcriptions for Coleridge, his enthusiasm for his poem re-kindled. The result was a sustained burst of creative activity and the completion of *The Prelude* a year later. Lastly, Cole-ridge could not have been untouched by the tender references to himself in the poem, for in the early version he is called the "most loving soul" and Wordsworth speaks of his "gentle spirit." When the poem appeared posthumously in 1850, many such references as these were either altered or omitted—mute testimony of the later estrangement between the two men.

The reading of *The Prelude* at Coleorton was for Coleridge a gratifying and inspiring experience. Here in this "portico" of *The Recluse* was the proper fulfillment of Wordsworth's genius and the promise of the grand philosophical poem to come. Coleridge's faith had been justified and his years of urging and entreaty had borne fruit.

In spite of the high hopes of both Wordsworth and Coleridge that they could renew the easy familiarity of earlier days, they were unable to do so. Wordsworth, now approaching middle age and a husband and father with domestic responsibilities, could no longer ignore the shortcomings of his friend, and while there was no diminution of intellectual intercourse, he began to pass moral judgment on Coleridge and to lose all hope that he would ever produce work of lasting significance. Coleridge, ever sensitive to a lack of genial feelings, did not, on the other hand, find the haven of tranquillity to which he had looked forward. His conduct, indeed, was enough to dis-gust one far less morally severe than Wordsworth. Revolted at the idea of returning to Mrs. Coleridge, he poured out in his notebooks passages of self-pity and frustration over Sara Hutchinson, and instead of pursuing a decisive course and assuming responsibility for his children, he failed to set him-self to any useful undertaking. If, then, Wordsworth was dis-appointed in his friend, Coleridge was equally unhappy, and the inevitable drifting apart of the two men had begun. Thus the Wordsworths, after a brief visit in London with Coleridge, returned to the Lake Country in the summer of 1807, despite their earlier resolution to live wherever Coleridge did, while Coleridge stayed on in London and Bristol for another year. The Wordsworths, however, still retained their high regard for Coleridge's genius. Writing from Grasmere to Lady Beaumont in April 1808 Dorothy remarked: "[Coleridge] is a wonderful creature, pouring out such treasures of thought and knowledge almost, we may say, without premeditation, and in language so eloquent."[54]

In the spring of 1808, Wordsworth intended to publish *The White Doe of Rylstone* with a preface mentioning Coleridge and acknowledging his indebtedness to the meter of *Christabel*, then, of course, still in manuscript; and he asked Coleridge, who was in London, to negotiate with Longman. Coleridge was not satisfied with the structure of the poem, and he strongly objected to the inclusion of the preface. Readers would instantly recognize the resemblance of the meter of *The White Doe* to that of Scott's *Lay of the Last Minstrel*, which had appeared in 1805. Nevertheless, they would hardly accept an acknowledgment of indebtedness to Coleridge's unpublished *Christabel*, and even if Wordsworth succeeded in establishing the "great *priority*" of the composition of *Christabel* to either Scott's poem or *The White Doe*, he would be accused of "a covert attack on Scott's Originality." In the midst of Coleridge's deliberations, however, Wordsworth wrote the publisher, withdrawing his poem from publication and stating that Coleridge had "proceeded without Authority."[55] When it finally appeared seven years later, it was without mention of Coleridge's *Christabel*.[56]

[54] *The Middle Years*, I, 199.
[55] *Samuel Taylor Coleridge*, by E. K. Chambers, Oxford, 1938, 347-54. (MS.)
[56] In a letter to Byron in 1815, Coleridge makes the following comment: "I have not learnt with what motive Wordsworth omitted the original advertisement prefixed to his White Doe, that the peculiar metre and mode of narration he had imitated from the Christabel." *Unpublished Letters*, II, 148. (MS.)

Coleridge first learned that the poem had been retracted by Wordsworth when he received a note from Longman enclosing Wordsworth's letter. He was rightly incensed at such high-handed treatment and in self-justification he declared in a letter to Wordsworth that he assuredly had been "commissioned" by him to make arrangements with the publisher. He outlined his criticism of both the poem and the preface, and he questioned whether *The White Doe* would enjoy a sale sufficient to relieve the "exceeding anxiety about pecuniary matters" of which Dorothy had reported. He deplored the recurrence of such financial fears as had harassed them at Racedown and referred to his plan to issue a periodical, *The Friend,* which he hoped would bring in "from 12 to 20 £ a week"[57] and thus free Wordsworth from monetary worries. The whole letter, indeed, combines an affectionate interest in Wordsworth's welfare with a vigorous, almost indignant, exculpation of himself.

In August 1808 Coleridge arrived at Grasmere, where he was to be an inmate of the Wordsworth household off and on for the next two years. He was filled with enthusiasm for *The Friend,* which, according to the prospectus, was to comprise weekly essays on moral, political, philosophical, and other subjects—and a veritable potpourri it turned out to be. Wordsworth entered into the undertaking, even helping to send off the prospectuses. But as time went by and Coleridge, who was away from Grasmere for four months in early 1809, failed to issue *The Friend,* Wordsworth gradually lost all hope of its success. At first he was content with such remarks as those he wrote to Poole: "I cannot say that Coleridge has been managing himself well; and therefore I would not have you disappointed if the 'Friend' should not last long";[58] but he was soon writing more emphatically. To Stuart, who was giving Coleridge financial assistance for *The Friend,* he reported: "Of

[57] E. K. Chambers, *op. cit.,* 350. (MS.)
[58] *The Middle Years,* I, 280.

the Friend and Coleridge I hear nothing, and am sorry to say I hope nothing. It is I think too clear that Coleridge is not sufficiently master of his own efforts to execute anything which requires a regular course of application to one object. I fear so—indeed I am of opinion that it is so—to my great sorrow."[59] And on the very day that the first number of *The Friend* appeared, he again notified Poole:

"I am sorry to say that nothing appears to me more desirable than that his periodical essay should never commence. It is in fact *impossible*—utterly impossible—that he should carry it on; and, therefore, better never begin it; far better, and if begun, the sooner it stops, also the better—the less will be the loss, and not greater the disgrace. . . . I give it to you as my deliberate opinion, formed upon proofs which have been strengthening for years, that he neither will nor can execute any thing of important benefit either to himself his family or mankind. Neither his talents nor his genius, mighty as they are, nor his vast information will avail him anything; they are all frustrated by a derangement in his intellectual and moral constitution. . . . Do not suppose that I mean to say from this that The Friend may not appear—it may—but it cannot go on for any length of time. I am *sure* it cannot."[60]

In contrast to this, Wordsworth, not having Coleridge at hand for consultation, yet still seeking his advice, wrote him that he "had a strong inclination to walk over to Keswick lately"; instead, he sent a full analysis of his proposed arrangement of his poems by classifications.[61] This arrangement, with some modifications, was followed in the next edition of his work. Such a scheme left no place for Coleridge's *Ancient Mariner* and the other poems printed without his name in all four editions of *Lyrical Ballads*. With characteristic indifference, he let eight years elapse before publishing them as his own compositions.

Apparently unconscious of the disillusionment of his friends,

[59] *Ibid.*, 319.   [60] *Ibid.*, 321.   [61] *Ibid.*, 304-9.

Coleridge was deeply concerned over the financial worries of the Wordsworths. A letter of Dorothy's written in May 1809 is most revealing:

"My Brother has begun to correct and add to the poem of the White Doe, and has been tolerably successful. . . . He has also made a resolution to write upon public affairs in the *Courier,* or some other newspaper, for the sake of getting money. . . . Coleridge, however, writes to desire that he will not withdraw himself from poetry, for he is assured that there will be no need of it, as he (Coleridge) can get money enough. I have, indeed, better hopes of him at present than I have had for this long time, laying together his own account of himself and the account which Mrs. C. gives us of him. . . . As to my Brother's writing for a newspaper I do not much like the thought of it; but . . . I know not how we can go on without his employing some portion of his time in that way."[62]

However generous this gesture on Coleridge's part may seem, it should be remembered that most of the time he was a member of the overflowing Wordsworth household, and that on week-ends his sons, Hartley and Derwent, swelled the family to fifteen persons. Small wonder, then, not only that Wordsworth was in severe financial straits but also that Coleridge felt himself to be under great obligations to him.

With the appearance of the first number of *The Friend* in June 1809 Coleridge returned to the Wordsworths, and Sara Hutchinson being on hand to act as his amanuensis, for a time things appeared more hopeful. Writing to Lady Beaumont in February 1810 Dorothy reports both on the slowness with which subscribers made their payments and on Coleridge's industry:

"Coleridge's spirits have been irregular of late. He was damped after the 20th number by the slow arrival of payments, and half persuaded himself that he ought not to go on. We laboured against such a resolve, and he seems determined to

[62] *Ibid.,* 294.

fight onwards. . . . Many people have not yet paid, merely from thoughtlessness, who, no doubt, will pay ere long; and the work cannot but answer in a pecuniary point of view, if there is not . . . a very great failure in the payments. By the great quantity of labour that he has performed since the commencement of *The Friend* you will judge that he has upon the whole been very industrious. . . . The fact is that he either does a great deal or nothing at all. . . . He has written a whole *Friend* more than once in two days. They are never re-transcribed, and he generally has dictated to Miss Hutchinson, who takes the words down from his mouth. . . . The essay of this week (No. 25) is by my brother."[63]

Despite Wordsworth's prognostications, *The Friend* ran to twenty-seven numbers, finally stopping on March 15, 1810. While he had regretted Coleridge's publication of the first issue, once the work was under way, he used his influence to insure its continuance and made contributions to it. But it failed, partly from mismanagement, partly from Coleridge's fitful habits of composition. Thus *The Friend* did not prove helpful in relieving Wordsworth's pecuniary distress, as Coleridge had hoped, and as it flickered out, the Wordsworths were more than ever convinced that Coleridge was not to be relied upon. While he was still a member of the household, Dorothy, writing to Catherine Clarkson on April 12, 1810, was probably expressing the views of the whole family:

"We have no hope of him. None that he will ever do anything more than he has already done. If he were not under our roof, he would be just as much the slave of stimulants as ever; and his whole time and thoughts, (except when he is reading and he reads a great deal), are employed in deceiving himself, and seeking to deceive others. . . . His love for . . . [Sara Hutchinson] is no more than a fanciful dream. Otherwise he would prove it by a desire to make her happy. No! He likes to have

[63] *Ibid.*, 358.

her about him as his own, as one devoted to him, but when she stood in the way of other gratifications it was all over."[64]

This is cruel and unsympathetic, however true it may be; but for the time being Coleridge was unaware that the personal attitude of the Wordsworths had undergone a radical change. He must have known that they undervalued his *Friend* —indeed, six years later he wrote that "from the beginning . . . nothing but cold water, or what is far worse, very cold praise, had been bestowed on it by my friends—even by Southey and Wordsworth"[65]—but he seems still not to have recognized the growing estrangement. Early in May 1810 he left the Wordsworths to join his family at Greta Hall and was never again a member of their household.

In October 1810, immediately after Coleridge had left the Lake Country for London, an open breach between him and Wordsworth occurred through the tale-bearing of Basil Montagu, but we may pass over the details of that melancholy affair. Stunned by the sudden realization that the Wordsworths had long ceased to love him, Coleridge suffered as he had never suffered before, and he attempted to banish from his heart the whole Wordsworth household, including Sara Hutchinson. Recognizing at last how unwise and how deleterious for himself his self-abnegating idolatry of Wordsworth had been, he poured out his agony in his notebooks and letters. On November 3, 1810, he recorded in his notebook:

"Now for fourteen years of my life, and those fourteen the very life of my life—and thro' a strange variety of states, situations, and circumstances, I am conscious to myself of having felt the most consummate friendship, in deed, word, and thought inviolate, for a man whose welfare never ceased to be far dearer to me than my own, and for whose fame I have been enthusiastically watchful, even at the price of alienating the affections of my benefactors,—and this during years, in which

[64] *Ibid.*, 366-7.
[65] *Unpublished Letters*, II, 178.

I stood single in my reverential admiration, and while for my own literary reputation I felt but a languid, at all events, a very desultory interest. I often warmed with indignation indeed, . . . that I passed among those, who were most disposed to think highly of me, for a deluded fanatic on account of my firmness in maintaining and my vehemence and enthusiasm in displaying the moral and intellectual superiority of my friend."[66]

In 1812 Coleridge and Wordsworth were superficially reconciled through the mediation of mutual friends. Not long afterwards, Coleridge reported to Poole: "You, perhaps, may . . . have heard . . . of the year-long Difference between me and Wordsworth—compared with the Sufferings of which all former Afflictions of my Life were less than Flea-bites—. . . A Reconciliation has taken place—but the *Feeling*, . . . after 15 years of such religious, almost Superstitious, Idolatry and Self-sacrifice—O No! No! that I fear, never can return. All outward actions, all inward Wishes, all Thoughts and Admirations, will be the same—*are* the same—but—aye there remains an immedicable *But*."[67]

Coleridge, indeed, saw at a glance how debilitating his "most enthusiastic, self-despising & alas! self-injuring Friendship"[68] for Wordsworth had been. Nor did he change his opinion. Years later he wrote with equal bitterness:

"Alas! during the prime manhood of my intellect I had nothing but cold water thrown on my efforts! . . . I have loved with enthusiastic self-oblivion those who have been so well pleased that I should, year after year, flow with a hundred nameless Rills into *their* Main Stream, that they could find nothing but cold praise and effective discouragement of every attempt of mine to roll onward in a distinct current of my own—who *admitted* that the Ancient Mariner, the Christabel, the Remorse, and *some* pages of the Friend were not without merit, but were

[66] T. M. Raysor, *loc. cit.*, 322.
[67] *Letters of Coleridge*, II, 612. (MS.)
[68] *Unpublished Letters*, II, 51. (MS.)

abundantly anxious to acquit their judgements of any blindness to the very numerous defects. Yet they *knew* that to *Praise,* as mere Praise, I was characteristically, almost constitutionally indifferent. In Sympathy alone I found at once Nourishment and Stimulus: and for Sympathy alone did my heart crave." And with belated recognition he noted the "mistake to which affectionate Natures are too liable. . .–the mistaking those who are desirous and well pleased to be loved *by* you for those who love you."[69] After Coleridge's domestication with the Gillmans at Highgate in 1816, he and Wordsworth occasionally met in London or at Highgate. But these were mere shadows of the former intimacy.

Once he recovered from his disillusionment following the quarrel with Wordsworth, Coleridge, under the warming influence and encouragement of other friends, roused himself, and despite the predictions of Wordsworth, produced a number of significant works during the next few years. Surprising as the conclusion seems, we must assume that the break in his relations with the Wordsworth family and Sara Hutchinson was in the long run beneficial to Coleridge. It freed him from an unhealthy dependence, it broke off a love affair which had harassed and tortured him, and it drove him to prove to himself and to the world that he was not a lost slave to opium. The publication of eight major works between 1813 and 1818 shows how really active he was. In the spring of 1815 he was busily occupied in gathering his poems for a collected edition, to which he proposed to add a preface expounding his theory of poetry.

In the meantime, in July 1814, Wordsworth had issued *The Excursion,* which as he declared in an apologetic preface, formed the second part of his projected philosophical poem, *The Recluse.* He explained that *The Recluse* would ultimately have three parts, and he included, as a "kind of *Prospectus* of the design and scope of the whole Poem," a hundred and seven

[69] *Letters of Coleridge,* ii, 696-7. (MS.)

lines from the conclusion to the First Book of Part I. Words-worth held high hopes for *The Excursion*. He noted with ob-vious pleasure any adulatory comments made by his friends, and it is easy to imagine how he awaited Coleridge's approval. After all, the two poets had drawn up the plan for *The Recluse* together, and *The Excursion* was in part the result of Cole-ridge's constant emphasis on a work of grand proportions. Then, too, Wordsworth suffered from the almost unanimous condemnation of the reviewers, particularly from the vicious attack in the *Edinburgh Review*, in which Jeffrey begins, "This will never do," and he naturally looked to his friends for favor-able judgment. Coleridge, however, was frankly disappointed with *The Excursion*,[70] and rather than offer criticism, for eight months he kept his views to himself, thus causing Wordsworth to doubt that he had even "read three pages of the poem."[71] Certainly, he did not intend to correspond with Wordsworth about *The Excursion*, but circumstances intervened. In April 1815 he wrote to Lady Beaumont, asking her to return his lines, *To William Wordsworth*, and telling her of his proposed pub-lication of his poems. Knowing full well that she would draw some "strange inference" if he made no comment on *The Ex-cursion*, he briefly summarized his feelings about it. Speaking

[70] In spite of his own dissatisfaction with *The Excursion*, Coleridge was "roused" by the "malignity, slander, hypocrisy, and self-contra-dicting Baseness" of Jeffrey's "infamous" review, which appeared in November 1814, and determined to "impeach" the author of it. Later he did so in the chapter "On the present mode of conducting critical jour-nals" in the *Biographia Literaria*. Coleridge shows that the reviewer was guilty "of arbitrary and . . . petulant verdicts, not seldom unsupported even by a single quotation from the work condemned." Even when ex-tracts are given they "are too often made without reference to any general grounds or rules from which the faultiness or inadmissibility of the qual-ities attributed may be deduced." Although Jeffrey cited passages of "eminent and original beauty" and owned that "beauties as great are scattered . . . throughout the whole," yet he "commenced his critique in vulgar exultation . . . with . . . 'This won't do!' " and after "consigning the author to the house of incurables," concluded "with a strain of rudest contempt . . . all this done without a single leading principle established or even announced." Shawcross, *op. cit.*, II, 90-2.
[71] *The Middle Years*, II, 622.

of *The Excursion* as a whole he said that "the tale of the ruined Cottage" he had "ever thought the finest Poem in our Language." Of the balance of the poem, "comparing it with any of the same or similar Length," he declared "that one half the number of it's Beauties would make all the beauties of all his Contemporary Poets collectively mount to the balance; but yet," he went on to add, "I do not think . . . it equal to" *The Prelude*. Since he found no flagging of genius in the poet, he concluded that Wordsworth had convinced himself of self-evident truths, and attached the importance and depth of his own "experiences, feelings, and reason . . . to doctrines and words, which come almost as Truisms . . . to others."[72]

Instead of returning Coleridge's poem, Lady Beaumont kept it, and it is still to be found among the Beaumont papers. Even more reprehensibly, she forwarded Coleridge's letter to Wordsworth, who wrote to Coleridge on May 22, 1815: "Let me beg out of kindness to me that you would relinquish the intention of publishing the Poem addressed to me after hearing *mine* to you. The commendation would be injurious to us both."[73] He then turned to Coleridge's remarks concerning *The Excursion* and asked that he cite the particular passages which had given rise to the opinion expressed in the letter to Lady Beaumont. Barely disguising his irritation, Wordsworth declared that he had "rather been perplexed than enlightened by your *comparative* censure," of this poem with *The Prelude,* and referring to Coleridge's charge that *The Excursion* expressed mere truisms, he replied: "One of my principal aims in the Ex^n: has

[72] *Letters of Coleridge,* II, 641-2. (MS.)
[73] *The Middle Years,* II, 669. In reply, Coleridge rather caustically swept aside Wordsworth's objection to the publication of the lines *To William Wordsworth*: "Your prudential Reasons would not have weighed with me, except as far as my name might haply injure your reputation/ for there is nothing in the Lines as far as your Powers are concerned, which I have not as fully expressed elsewhere—and I hold it a miserable cowardice to withhold a deliberate opinion only because the man is alive." *Letters of Coleridge,* II, 645. (MS.) Actually, Coleridge, having a rude draft in his possession, published his poem in *Sibylline Leaves.*

been to put the commonplace truths, of the human affections especially, in an interesting point of view; and rather to remind men of their knowledge, as it lurks inoperative and unvalued in their own minds, than to attempt to convey recondite or refined truths.[74] Pray point out to me the most striking instances where I have failed, in producing poetic effect by an overfondness for this practice, or through inability to realize my wishes."[75]

In answer to Wordsworth, Coleridge first pointed out that letters are a poor substitute "for a viva voce examination of a

[74] Coleridge, commenting on this statement of Wordsworth's, replied: "This I supposed to have been" your object "in your two Volumes of Poems [1815 edition], as far as was desirable, or possible. . . . How can common truths be made permanently interesting but by being *bottomed* in our common natures?" *Letters of Coleridge*, II, 649-50. (MS.)

[75] *The Middle Years*, II, 669-70. Coleridge, in answer, assured Wordsworth that he would "in two or at farthest three days—. . . dismissing all comparison either with . . . [*The Prelude*], or with the imagined Plan of the Recluse, state fairly my main Objections to the Excursion as it is. But it would have been alike unjust both to you and to myself, if I had led you to suppose that any disappointment, I may have felt, arose wholly or chiefly from the Passages, I do not like—or from the Poem considered irrelatively." *Letters of Coleridge*, II, 650. (MS.) The days of reserving his critical comments for Wordsworth's ear alone were over, however, and it was not until 1817, in the *Biographia Literaria*, that Coleridge cited passages from *The Excursion*, or considered the poem "irrelatively." In the chapter on the characteristic defects of Wordsworth's poetry in the *Biographia* Coleridge gives some of the faults of *The Excursion*. "In a *poem*, the characters . . . amid the strongest individualization, must still remain representative. . . . Is there one word, for instance, attributed to the pedlar in the 'Excursion,' characteristic of a *pedlar*? One sentiment, that might not more plausibly . . . have proceeded from any wise and beneficent old man, of a rank or profession in which the language of learning and refinement are natural and to be expected? Need the rank have been at all particularized, where nothing follows which the knowledge of that rank is to explain or illustrate? When on the contrary this information renders the man's language, feelings, sentiments, and information a riddle, which must itself be solved by episodes of anecdote?" He concludes that "all the admirable passages interposed . . . might, with trifling alterations, have been far more appropriately, and with far greater verisimilitude, told of a poet in the character of a poet." He cites examples of "minute matters of fact" that might better appear in obituary notices, and as instances of "prolixity, repetition, and an eddying, instead of progression, of thought," he points specifically to the "first eighty lines of the Sixth Book of the Excursion." Shawcross, *op. cit.*, II, 106-9.

81

Work with it's Author, Line by Line." Referring to his criticism as given in the letter to Lady Beaumont, Coleridge said "that *comparatively* with . . . [*The Prelude*] the excursion, as far as it was new to me, had disappointed my expectations." He felt that he could best explain his disappointment by recalling to Wordsworth's mind what his expectations were. He supposed that *The Prelude* "was as the ground-plat and the Roots, out of which the Recluse was to have sprung." While he expected the two poems to form "one compleat Whole" yet each would be "not only a distinct but a different Work." *The Prelude*, he considered, was *The Excursion*, and with its completion Wordsworth would then begin *The Recluse*, his great philosophical poem: "In the very Pride of confident Hope I looked forward to the Recluse, as the *first* and *only* true Philosophical Poem in existence. Of course, I expected the Colors, Music, imaginative Life, and Passion of *Poetry*; but the matter and arrangement of *Philosophy*—not doubting from the advantages of the Subject that the Totality of a System was not only capable of being harmonized with, but even calculated to aid, the unity . . . of a *Poem*."[76] Coleridge then fully outlined what he believed was to have been the plan for *The Recluse*—a plan of staggering proportions, which appears earlier in this chapter.[77] With such high expectations, Coleridge was justified in his feeling of bewilderment and disappointment on reading *The Excursion*, which fell far short of the comprehensive design he and Wordsworth had laid down.

We do not know how Wordsworth responded to this forthright and manly letter. He must have been considerably disconcerted, and Coleridge's unqualified disapproval may have been in part responsible for his failure to go on with *The Recluse*. Its non-fulfillment troubled his conscience for many years, and as Miss Darbishire so aptly says, "all that was accomplished of the great philosophical poem . . . was a Prelude

[76] *Letters of Coleridge*, II, 644-648. (MS.)
[77] See pp. 51-3.

to the main theme, and an Excursion from it."[78] For his part, Coleridge never again explained, either in his letters or in print, the grounds of his disappointment with *The Excursion*. In the *Biographia Literaria* the poem is treated without reference to *The Prelude* or to the plan for *The Recluse*.

Coleridge did not change his opinion of *The Excursion*. In 1822, for example, Crabb Robinson reports him as censuring Wordsworth for "a vulgar attachment to orthodoxy in its literal sense" and asserting that "the latter end of the *Excursion* . . . is distinguished from the former." Coleridge, Robinson notes further, "can ascertain by internal evidence the recent from the early compositions among his works. He reproaches Wordsworth with a disregard to the mechanism of his verse, and in general insinuates a decline of his faculties."[79]

Again, in 1832, Coleridge said he had often wished that the first two books of *The Excursion* had been published separately as "The Deserted Cottage," since "they would have formed, what indeed they are, one of the most beautiful poems in the language."[80]

It seems likely that the correspondence with Wordsworth concerning *The Excursion* led Coleridge to expand his proposed preface to his poems into the *Biographia Literaria* and to incorporate into it not only his examination of the Preface to *Lyrical Ballads* but the critique of Wordsworth's poetry as well. Moreover, Coleridge's surprise at finding Wordsworth's definitions of imagination and fancy, as presented in the Preface to the 1815 edition of his poems, so "widely different" from his own,[81] may have been responsible for his extensive elucidation of those terms in the *Biographia Literaria*. Coleridge, indeed, expresses the divergence of opinion in that work: "It was Mr. Wordsworth's purpose to consider the in-

[78] *The Poet Wordsworth,* by Helen Darbishire, Oxford, 1950, 90.
[79] *Coleridge's Miscellaneous Criticism,* ed. by T. M. Raysor, London, 1936, 397.
[80] *Table Talk,* II, 69.
[81] *Unpublished Letters,* II, 143.

fluences of fancy and imagination as they are manifested in poetry, and from the different effects to conclude their diversity in kind; while it is my object to investigate the seminal principle, and then from the kind to deduce the degree."[82]

To deal fully with the criticism of Wordsworth in the *Biographia Literaria* lies outside the province of this chapter, but enough evidence has been adduced to show that Coleridge developed most of his critical ideas about Wordsworth's work during their long association and that his published comments were merely a public expression of what he had long felt and in many cases of what he had actually written to friends or said to Wordsworth. This is especially true of his criticism of the Preface to *Lyrical Ballads*. With certain parts of that Preface he had no quarrel. He rejected as strenuously as Wordsworth did, for example, the false poetic diction of his immediate predecessors. He believed, nevertheless, that "the unexampled opposition which Mr. Wordsworth's writings have been since doomed to encounter"[83] was due in great measure to the Preface, and he makes short work of Wordsworth's statements concerning the source of poetic diction. He shows that in Wordsworth's best poems "the persons introduced are by no means taken *from low or rustic life* in the common acceptation of those words,"[84] and he proceeds to contradict, both in theory and by illustration from Wordsworth's poems, the assertion that the language of rural characters has been adopted. Since "the best part of human language, properly so called, is derived from reflection on the acts of the mind itself,"[85] and since Wordsworth's "diction, next to that of Shakespeare and Milton, appears . . . of all others the most *individualized* and characteristic,"[86] the irresistible conclusion is that Wordsworth does not derive his language from men in low and rustic life.

[82] Shawcross, *op. cit.*, ɪ, 64. [83] *Ibid.*, 51.
[84] *Ibid.*, ɪɪ, 31. [85] *Ibid.*, 39-40.
[86] *Ibid.*, 77.

84

In controverting Wordsworth's assertion that there is no essential difference between the language of prose and that of metrical composition, Coleridge dismisses as self-evident the fact that certain lines in either poetry or prose may be interchangeable and insists that "in the language of a serious poem . . . [there is] an arrangement both of words and sentences, and a use and selection of . . . *figures of speech*, both as to their kind, their frequency, and their occasions, which on a subject of equal weight would be vicious and alien in correct and manly prose."[87] Likewise, he clearly shows that meter is not superadded to poetry but is an organic part of it. In masterly fashion he adduces several reasons for his contention and rests his case on "the practice of the best poets, of all countries and in all ages, as *authorizing* the opinion . . . that . . . there may be, is, and ought to be an essential difference between the language of prose and of metrical composition."[88]

The critique dealing with Wordsworth's poetry looks at first sight like a weighing of the faults and virtues of the poems themselves, and indeed, it may be so treated, but certainly Coleridge considered it to be grounded upon philosophical principles. This critique must be read in full to be appreciated. It is clear and pointed and lacks the digressive tendency of most of Coleridge's prose. Even an enumeration of the points pro and con, without the inclusion of the illustrations from the poems, will reveal his remarkable critical acumen, as well as the relationship of his criticism to his theory of imagination. As defects in Wordsworth's poetry Coleridge lists "the INCONSTANCY of the *style*," a "*matter-of-factness*," "an undue predilection for the *dramatic* form," "occasional prolixity, repetition, and an eddying, instead of progression, of thought," and "thoughts and images too great for the subject"; and as excellences he finds "an austere purity of language, . . . a perfect appropriateness of the words to the meaning," "a correspondent weight and sanity of the Thoughts and Sentiments,"

[87] *Ibid.*, 49.   [88] *Ibid.*, 56-7.

"the sinewy strength and originality of single lines and para-
graphs," "the perfect truth of nature in his images and descriptions," "a meditative pathos, a union of deep and subtle
thought with sensibility," and "the gift of IMAGINATION
in the highest and strictest sense of the word. . . . In imaginative power, he stands nearest of all modern writers to Shakespeare and Milton; and yet in a kind perfectly unborrowed
and his own."[89]

Coleridge knew that Wordsworth would be displeased with
the *Biographia Literaria,* but in contrast to his earlier defer-
ence, he had written that work with independence of purpose.
To several of his friends he justified his convictions. On July 29,
1815, he wrote to Dr. Brabant: "I have just finished it. . . . I
have given a full account (*raisonné*) of the controversy concerning Wordsworth's Poems and Theory, in which my name
has been so constantly included. I have no doubt that Wordsworth will be displeased, but I have done my duty to myself
and to the public, in, as I believe, completely subverting the
theory and in proving that the poet himself has never acted
on it except in particular stanzas, which are the blots of his
composition."[90]

Two years later, in a copy of the second volume of the *Biographia,* he wrote the following note to his son: "In this volume,
my dear Derwent, I have compressed all I know of the principles of a sober yet not ungenial Criticism: and most anxiously
have I avoided all mere *assertion*—all *opinion* not followed or
preceded by the reasons, on which it has been grounded. Of
one thing I am distinctly conscious, viz. that my main motive
and continued impulse was to secure, as far as in me lay, an
intelligent admiration of Mr Wordsworth's Poems—and while
I frankly avowed what I deemed defects, and why I deemed
them so, yet to evince how *very* trifling they were not only in

[89] *Ibid.,* 97-124.
[90] *Westminster and Foreign Quarterly Review,* N.S., Vol. xxxvii, No.
2 (April 1, 1870), 361.

importance but even in the proportional space occupied by
them; and lastly to satisfy at once a favorite wish as well as
favorite conviction of my own, which I cannot better express
than by adopting the following stanza of old Gascoigne's in
application to Wordsworth's Genius.

> Lo! As a Hawk that soareth tow'rd the sky
> And climbs aloft for solace of his wing,
> The greater gate she getteth up on high,
> The truer stoupe she makes at any thing.

"If in so doing I have offended where I should most wish
and did most expect to please, it is but one of many proofs that
I have been too apt to judge of the feelings of others by my
own."[91]

To H. F. Cary, Coleridge pointed out that "any feeling of
personal partiality would rather lead me to doubts and dis-
satisfactions respecting a particular work in proportion as it
might possibly occasion me to overrate the man"; and referring
to Wordsworth, he continued: "If, indeed, I do estimate too
highly what I deem the characteristic excellencies of Wordsworth's poems, it results from a congeniality of taste without
a congeniality in the productive power; but to the faults and
defects I have been far more alive than his detractors, even
from the first publication of the 'Lyrical Ballads,' though for
a long course of years my opinions were sacred to his own
ear."[92]

Finally, in a much more personal letter to Thomas Allsop
of December 2, 1818, Coleridge said he had "long and faith-
fully . . . acted on the maxim, never to admit the *faults* of a
work of Genius to those who denied or were incapable of
feeling and understanding the *Beauties*: not from wilful partiality but as well knowing that in *saying* truth I should to such
Critics *convey* falsehood." Referring to his *Biographia Liter-*

---

[91] *Times Literary Supplement,* July 3, 1948. (MS.)
[92] *Letters of Coleridge,* II, 677-8.

aria he continued: "If in one instance (in my Literary Life) I have appeared to deviate from this rule, first, it was not till the fame of the Writer (which I had been for 14 years successively toiling, like a second Ali, to build up) had been established: and secondly and chiefly, with the purpose and, I may safely add, with the *effect* of rescuing the necessary task from Malignant Defamers and in order to set forth the excellences and the trifling proportion which the Defects bore to the excellences."[93]

However just the strictures on the Preface and the critique on Wordsworth's poetry may have been, Wordsworth did not look with favor on the *Biographia Literaria,* and the following excerpt from Crabb Robinson's diary for December 4, 1817, shows how deeply wounded he was: "Coleridge's book has given him [Wordsworth] no pleasure, and he finds just fault with Coleridge for professing to write about himself and writing merely about Southey and Wordsworth. With the criticism on the poetry too he is not satisfied. The praise is extravagant and the censure inconsiderate. I recollected hearing Hazlitt say that Wordsworth would not forgive a single censure mingled with however great a mass of eulogy."[94]

Coleridge's estimate of Wordsworth covers a period of about twenty years, if we ignore a few stray remarks in later letters and in *Table Talk,* and culminates in the criticisms included in the *Biographia Literaria* in 1817. In the years before the quarrel, Coleridge protested vigorously against certain aspects of Wordsworth's critical theory as expressed in the Preface to *Lyrical Ballads,* and he seems to have been so obsessed with Wordsworth's ability to produce a philosophical poem that after 1800, certainly, he came to ignore the importance of the "little poems." Then in 1815, with the memories not only of the years of happy comradeship but also of their bitter sequel crowding in upon him, he endeavored to set down his critical views in an impersonal way. Though he maintained his critical

[93] *Ibid.,* 697. (MS.)   [94] Edith J. Morley, *op. cit.,* I, 213.

integrity and did not allow his personal feelings to sway his judgment, his criticisms of Wordsworth in the *Biographia Literaria* leave much unsaid. His discussion of the Preface is mostly destructive and fails to take into account the significance of its contributions to critical theory. The critique of Wordsworth's poetry does not consider the broader, philosophical implications of the poet's thought. There is, of course, no criticism of *The Prelude*, for he could not without impropriety discuss a poem still in manuscript. Nevertheless, Coleridge successfully refuted two central fallacies in the Preface, examined Wordsworth's poetry with incisive brilliance, and set the criticism of Wordsworth on the right track.

The *Biographia Literaria*, however, appeared after Wordsworth's great poetic years were over; and though it really established his reputation, of more importance to the poet himself were the understanding, sympathy, and help given so generously by Coleridge at the beginning of their association. And no one was more conscious of his indebtedness than Wordsworth himself. In some deleted lines apparently intended as a beginning for Book Two of *The Prelude*, Coleridge is tenderly referred to:

> Friend of my heart and Genius
> . . . I seem'd to need thy cheering voice,[95]

and in 1832, not long before Coleridge's death, Wordsworth said that Coleridge "and my beloved sister are the two beings to whom my intellect is most indebted."[96] Sir Walter Raleigh sums up the matter very well: "The chief benefit he [Wordsworth] received from Coleridge's friendship lay, after all, in the strength that comes from early appreciation."[97] Coleridge is to be remembered, therefore, for the inspiration he afforded Wordsworth in the development of his poetic genius, for being

[95] Helen Darbishire, *op. cit.*, 91. [96] *The Later Years*, II, 625.
[97] Raleigh, *op. cit.*, 85.

his best defender during the long period of non-recognition and ridicule, for reading and evaluating his work with penetrating insight, for anticipating the twentieth-century estimate of him, and for revealing something of his rich though hidden personality.

WILLIAM WORDSWORTH: NOTES
TOWARD AN UNDERSTANDING OF POETRY

BY JOHN CROWE RANSOM

OUR poet was one of the giants. We cannot say less, for Wordsworth did what Burns and Blake could not do: he reversed the direction of English poetry in a bad time, and revitalized it. But in order to do this he had to speculate upon what was possible, and what was advantageous, by virtue of the very constitution of a poetic action; he had to study poetry as well as write it. He was driven to a conception of poetry which was more radical, or thoroughgoing, than that of any of his predecessors, but it justified itself in his own poetic production. It is Wordsworth's innovations in the theory upon which I should like to offer some notes, as my tribute to the poet: in the theory, because he theorized as well as practised; and notes, because my impressions are speculative and imperfect, and in what has always been an area of speculation do not aspire anyway to be demonstrative.

The first notes have to do with the famous doctrine of poetic diction as laid down in the Preface. I had written, the "notorious" Preface, for it was a monstrous indiscretion, such as no other important poet ever committed so far as I know: giving his enemies two targets instead of one. There was a saving rightness in it, but its valor was that of an innocent, while the stubbornness which kept on republishing it indicated a man with a philanthropic intention.

In the Preface Wordsworth declares that the language of poetry is not different from the language of prose. He enters qualifications, however. He calls it once the language of "good" prose, and again the language of prose "when prose is well written." Nor does he claim that this neutral language is the language of all poetry, but that it is the language of much of the best poetry, and especially the language which he has made the staple of his own poetry. I mention these reservations, because I would not have it thought that Coleridge, who ridiculed the statement, must be in the right because he had the last word. Coleridge writes about it in the *Biographia Literaria* just after Wordsworth, in 1815, had finally published a new edition without putting the famous Preface in front of it; and Coleridge reads Wordsworth a long and weary lecture about an unqualified identification of the languages of prose and poetry which Wordsworth had not made. One is tempted to feel that Coleridge is determined to praise Wordsworth's poetry, as he has always done, but in the matter of poetic theory is pretty confident that the honors will lie with himself. And indeed Coleridge's critical writing was much more supple and professional, better organized and documented, than Wordsworth's. It has been of permanent influence upon poetic theory. Nevertheless, he did not write like an acute critic about poetic diction; and, for that matter, when it came to the point of discovering the three occasional faults in Wordsworth's poetry, and the six excellences which were frequent, we do not find Coleridge using incisive critical principles, but perfunctory and academic ones which scarcely convey the sense that this poetry was revolutionary.

Wordsworth documents his contention about prose diction skimpily, by citing a single poem and disposing of it quickly. But if we will consider what he does not say along with what he says, it will give us a good deal of Wordsworth's mind. To find the diction he approves he takes an eighteenth-century poem, so that we are not surprised if his approval does not extend to the whole poem. It is Gray's sonnet on the death of Richard West, which contains in some form the Wordsworthian tender feelings toward nature, and by all means a Wordsworthian "elementary" passion of grief for a friend. Here is the poem:

> In vain to me the smiling mornings shine,
> And reddening Phoebus lifts his golden fire:
> The birds in vain their amorous descant join,
> Or cheerful fields resume their green attire.
> These ears, alas! for other notes repine;
> A different object do these eyes require;
> My lonely anguish melts no heart but mine;
> And in my breast the imperfect joys expire;
> Yet morning smiles the busy race to cheer,
> And new-born pleasure brings to happier men;
> The fields to all their wonted tribute bear;
> To warm their little loves the birds complain.
> I fruitless mourn to him that cannot hear,
> And weep the more because I weep in vain.

In this sonnet the octet composes nicely by having its base-lines AB rhymed three times, while the sestet composes by having its base-lines CD rhymed twice: ABABABAB, CDCDCD. In the first half of the octet the speaker represents the morning with its sunshine, the birds, and the fields, as trying by turns to cheer him with their small joys. In the second half of the octet he resists them, on the ground that his ears are listening for other sounds and his eyes looking for other sights, while his heart has an anguish they cannot understand, so that their imperfect joys expire within his breast (perhaps before they reach his heart of hearts). In the first four lines of the sestet the amiable objects try him again, perhaps with more spirit, and in almost the original order: the morning, the fields, and the birds. In the concluding two lines he dismisses them once more with the important specification that he mourns to "him that cannot hear" and weeps to one who is not there to comfort him. This is about as graceful in design as the elegiac mode can well afford to be.

In printing the poem Wordsworth italicizes certain lines as

follows: all the speaker's words about himself which make the second quatrain, except its first line, so that we have:

> *A different object do these eyes require;*
> *My lonely anguish melts no heart but mine;*
> *And in my breast the imperfect joys expire;*

and all the speaker's words about himself at the end:

> *I fruitless mourn to him that cannot hear,*
> *And weep the more because I weep in vain.*

His comment is in a single sentence: "It will easily be perceived, that the only part of this Sonnet which is of any value is the lines printed in Italics; it is equally obvious, that, except in the rhyme, and in the use of the single word 'fruitless' for fruitlessly, which is so far a defect, the language of these lines does in no respect differ from that of prose."

Now the italicized lines are not a bad illustration of his point, though Coleridge picks at them. It is something for Wordsworth to have found them in a poem by Gray, whom he introduced as "more than any other man curiously elaborate in the structure of his own poetic diction." Really there was "flesh and blood," as Wordsworth required, in the academic young poet who, at twenty-six, mourning for his old friend and schoolmate, was like Milton, at twenty-nine, mourning for Henry King; though the later poet's *Lycidas* turns out to be a very small affair. The lines in which he expresses his grief are "manly," to use another Wordsworthian term, and especially, as compared with the lines about the natural objects, they are plain. Undoubtedly it is Wordsworth's principle that the situation has such dignity in itself as not to need the elaborate eighteenth-century diction to support it, nor the handsome reinforcements furnished by simile and metaphor as recommended by the rhetorics. In this particular poem the dead friend's character is not explored, but there is no time for it, and at any rate we have in every line of the speaker about him

94

the expression of his own feeling; for the subject's feeling belongs in this style as well as the treatment of the object. The one line which Wordsworth rejects from this part is where the subject's ears are said to "repine"; the tropology is foolish there, though in the next line it seems proper for his eyes to "require."

And now the reasons for Wordsworth's dissatisfaction with the other lines. The Phoebus business of course is out. But otherwise it is touching, in some degree, that the natural objects seem to solicit the mourner to partake of their joy, and in saying "joy" the poet is in the heart of Wordsworth's own vocabulary. But the objects are too pretty, they are too petty, and the fact is that they are too meanly regarded altogether. In one of the happiest moments of his life—and it was in 1800, the very year of the first publication of the Preface—we find Wordsworth come to live at last at Grasmere to pursue his dedicated career, and writing a passage about the surpassing beauty of the region in which he declares solemnly: "On Nature's invitation do I come." But this was the opening of a long poem in which the poet assigns to nature the most magnificent attentions to man; we shall see something of this.

We will imagine also that he did not like the idea of Gray's having his speaker decline the solicitations of the natural objects, poor though they might be; that was "sullen" of him, as Wordsworth would have said. In the poem *Ruth*, the English girl who has been won by the "Youth from Georgia's shore" is abandoned by her husband even before embarkation for America, and left to lead the life of a vagrant; and what is her response to nature now? She was won originally by her husband's account of the charms of his country, being sensitive to those of her own; and now we read:

> The engines of her pain, the tools
> That shaped her sorrow, rocks and pools,
> And airs that gently stir
> The vernal leaves—she loved them still;

Nor ever taxed them with the ill
Which had been done to her.

It was likewise with Michael himself, in that finer poem which
tells how the old shepherd had seen his son Luke go out to
seek his fortune, but not till he was sworn to return with
means to save the humble estate, and strength to help his
father complete the building of the stone sheepfold; and how
finally the old man has the news that Luke has plunged into
the dissolute ways of the city and fled for his misdeeds beyond
the seas. Nevertheless

                              among the rocks
He went, and still looked up to sun and cloud,
And listened to the wind; and, as before,
Performed all kinds of labour for his sheep,
And for the land, his small inheritance;

so that perhaps we feel meanly relieved, a little easier in the
presence of such magnanimity, when we are told that though
he went as usual to the sheepfold,

                              'tis believed by all
That many and many a day he thither went,
And never lifted up a single stone.

  The plain diction or prose-poetry diction which Wordsworth defends on principle, and adopts for himself, is evidently that which registers factually a human passion for a
concrete object. It is time to introduce that word "concrete."
It is an ill-favored word, but I cannot think that as critics we
can do without it. Modern philosophy has no other word which
stands so squarely for the natural object in its full character.
It is valuable for ontologists to have the word to denote that
plenum of the natural world which is so much denser than
our appetites need it to be, and denser than our intellect can
grasp when it would lay down in science the laws of nature.
It has even become corrective of modern science, which would

otherwise attach too absolute a reality to these laws. The name
to cite here, I should think, is that of Alfred North Whitehead,
whose *Science and the Modern World* shows how far the
science of the eighteenth century had failed to be an account
of the world which we familiarly sense. His name is the better
for my purpose because it is well known to Wordsworthians;
he has a chapter that pays great honor to Wordsworth as the
man who broke through the Great Chain of Being which was
becoming more and more the attenuated or abstracted being
of a mechanistic universe. And his word for the object of
Wordsworth's vision is concreteness; he might have preferred
to say "prehensive unity," but that would probably have
estranged the Wordsworthians. Wordsworth knew that the
poet always seeks concreteness. He knew also that it is the
animal or appetitive faculties, and science and business their
instruments, which deal with the abstractions, and a faculty
quite different which is interested in concretions. Our appetitive business with a concretion is to find some use to abstract
from it, and then to abandon it; but when we are out of the
dominion of our appetitive urgencies we engage with a concretion by fixing upon it our passion, or our affections large and
small. And thus a considerable part of our history is written
round concreteness as such. It is in exception to our animal
economy, to all appearances, but this is our actual behavior.
In choosing to deal directly with the natural concretions,
and with the feelings which engage with them, Wordsworth
was willing to throw away most of the tropology with which
poetry was commonly identified. But we may put this quite
clearly in terms which we owe to Professor I. A. Richards;[1]
they are now in wide usage. Wordsworth proposed to stick
to the *tenor* of his situation, and have little recourse to ex-
traneous *vehicles*. This defines the "good prose" which he
liked. It would not be the merely utilitarian prose, but the
prose to be found in sermons, in literary essays, above all in

[1] *The Philosophy of Rhetoric,* London, 1936.

our time in prose fictions, and wherever else the style develops the "concretions of nature" rather than the lean "concretions of discourse." For some two years I have felt deeply grateful to Wordsworth for giving his authority to this special kind of language. Perhaps it will improve our perspective on the linguistic performance of the poet, and not be a mere impertinence, if I list the several general devices which I find peculiar to the poetic language, including of course the prose-poetry language favored by Wordsworth. The list is crude, but I have been testing it over several years, and the devices seem really distinct.

1. This is the one in which I feel confirmed by Wordsworth. The device consists in using Singular Terms, or perhaps we might call them Spreaders; i.e., words and phrases which explore the vivid concreteness in the objects and events, even while seeming to prosecute a discourse in logical terms which would refer only to their uses. This is the primary device in any stylebook, and it richly deserves study. It is the way in which sensibility is put to work. I name it first, because its reference is entirely within the tenor. But I came to it last.

2. Dystactical Terms, or Rufflers; where a logical confusion is deliberately cultivated. The terms would be such as inversions, alterations in the idiom, ambiguities and obscurities, faulty series, condensations and ellipses, omission of rational connectives. They too stick to the given or tenor in a sense, but they return it to its original inchoate state of nature, so to speak, where we have to look to find the logical connections. Perhaps the assumption is that while doing so we will have to receive a substantial sense of the original concretions. This device has perhaps as many varieties named in the rhetorics as the one which follows; and Longinus is a critic who knows how to pin them down.

3. Metaphorical Terms, or Importers; where vehicle is introduced. By way of analogy or association of ideas, foreign objects are brought into the situation. This is the most spectacular

98

of the linguistic devices, and easiest to remark. Doctor Johnson enunciated the rule of practice: "A simile, to be perfect, must both illustrate and ennoble." That is to say, the vehicle must have good logical excuse to get in, and its objective content must have the same sense with respect to its powerful affects as the tenor into which it is introduced; so that it both extends the concretion and fortifies our feelings toward the original object.

4. Meters. Fundamentally, we must believe, they mean to enlarge the poetic concretion by introducing the phonetic values which belong to the medium and are independent of the semantic referent. Wordsworth said good things about the functions of meter without saying this primary thing; but he did not employ our terms concreteness and concretion.[2]

Wordsworth is able to compose many lyrics and longer poems by employing spreaders (1) and meters (4) alone. It is the first of his great innovations. Poetry of that kind was not unheard of before Wordsworth, but it did not exist in important poetry on this scale. Many readers are repelled by the

---

[2] Linguistic devices such as I have listed seem well within the repertory of every accomplished poet. Wordsworth made use of importers (3) and even a low grade of rufflers (2) when he wished; and of course there is that large chapter of his achievement which consists in the five hundred sonnets, which began with his listening one day (it was May 21, 1802) to Dorothy's reading of Milton's sonnets; in the sonnets there is a great extension of Wordsworth's tropology, and also of the topical range of his verse.

I should like to remark at least in a subnote that Santayana has given us the term "concretion of nature" to mean the natural object itself as given to the sensibility; and the term "concretion of discourse" to mean the operational rule by which we abstract from the sensible objects those aspects that are fitted logically for our use. I think there must also be distinguished a third concretion, the "concretion of art," which is different from either. Thus in a poem the total concretion realized will usually combine a concretion of discourse and certain concretions of nature as established within the field of operation by spreaders (1) and rufflers (2), plus an increment of exotic foreign content as established by importers (3); plus a completely new dimension of content as established by meters (4). The poetic concretion is of maximum comprehensiveness in the kinds of content, and probably must be regarded as a concretion which can be unified only within the spread of the imagination.

shortage in rufflers (2) and importers (3), which they have
learned to expect of poets, and which in other poets they have
found giving to verse its greatest brilliance. They regard
Wordsworth's poetry as too plain; and indeed we must think
of it as the plain style. Probably it is not so plain absolutely
as comparatively. The plain style sticks to its tenor, but there
may be a great range of sensibility carrying it on and establishing vivid and abundant content. The stylist can achieve
his distinction here as well as anywhere else. If there is still
a tendency to flatness, comparatively speaking, it will incline
to relieve this impression by registrations of feeling which the
showy styles do not commonly like to affect. And Wordsworth
himself attached great importance, evidently greater than
other poets have done, to the meters, as a wonderful instru-
ment of concretion. My own idea is that many of us for the
first time, when we were young, discovered in the poetry of
Wordsworth what poetry was; but turned from him as we
became experienced in other poetry of greater virtuosity; and
through some need felt in our maturity have finally come back
to him with admiration for the purity of his style. The test
poem for me is *Michael*. No part of it is less plain or more plain
than the lines I have quoted. I have wavered between resistance and participation till at last it has (at this writing) won
me. It has a kind of virtuosity of its own, which consists in its
relentless understatement (by poetical standards) of the occasion, where other poets are virtuosos by overstatement, over-
writing, aiming perhaps to overwhelm us with their "fine
excess." In *Resolution and Independence* the style is less severe,
the imagination is stirring as if about to spring into metaphor
though it stops short, and the musical effect is especially lux-
urious. *The Old Cumberland Beggar* is on the order of
Michael. The shorter and more lyrical poems do not exercise
us so much by their denial. Yet *I wandered lonely as a cloud,
The Solitary Reaper,* and *To the Cuckoo* are almost entirely

in plain style. And among the Lucy poems I will quote the brief last one:

> A slumber did my spirit seal;
>   I had no human fears:
> She seemed a thing that could not feel
>   The touch of earthly years.
>
> No motion has she now, no force;
>   She neither hears nor sees;
> Rolled round in earth's diurnal course
>   With rocks, and stones, and trees.

This is technically very different from those other lines about Lucy, where she was

> A violet by a mossy stone
>   Half hidden from the eye!
> Fair as a star, when only one
>   Is shining in the sky.

It is finer; of more powerful concretion. And it has a tone most unusual in Wordsworth, if I am not mistaken. The language of the second stanza, with its "motion," "force," and "earth's diurnal course," is very close to the language of Newtonian physics against which, at least as a description of man's relation to his universe, Wordsworth is said by Whitehead to have been the chief rebel. In that case we have here a savage irony. Professor Cleanth Brooks is most adept among critics in spotting ironies, and has even found them in Wordsworth's *Ode*, though I imagine this poet at large must offer lean hunting in that species of game; but I should covet his remark on this second stanza. To me it seems to say: How right are these mechanic philosophers, for Lucy herself is in the grip of their forces and revolutions—now that she is dead! Irony and satire would be well within the scope of the poetry of the tenor or fact. But the greatest locus of the plain style, of course, must be *The Prelude*. Whether we read it for psychological narrative, or natural description, or philosophy, we find a magnificence which many times is sustained at great length.

The remaining notes will have to do with another originality of Wordsworth's: his doctrine concerning the love of nature as the poetic theme. We must look now not at the Preface but at the formidable *Prelude,* which is poetic theory in verse. Does a man really love nature, and how may that be, and what good comes of it? *The Prelude* of course is a long spiritual autobiography in which Wordsworth memorizes with great fullness his own encounters with nature and comments on them. He had grown up in the love of nature; he had gone out into the world of affairs and come to grief; he had attended with a young man's generous fervor upon the French Revolution, and suffered disillusionment; he had tried to work his way out of his sickness by intellectual decisions, and failed; and in the end it took a return to the nature of the early days to heal him. That is the point to which the narrative of *The Prelude* brings him, at age thirty-five, after an unusual range of vital experience.

There are some commonplaces of knowledge which I shall not argue. Evidently it is natural enough for a child to love nature, and there is no reason for him to outgrow it. It is natural too, and important, to love man, but Wordsworth for the unity of his doctrine prefers to think that this comes about as one of the consequences of loving nature—in whose tone he thinks he can catch "the still, sad music of humanity." I agree with Professor Lionel Trilling that it is natural for the child to love man even in the first place, especially man in the person of his mother. Wordsworth would not deny this. But it is especially from the love of nature that the peculiar Wordsworthian benefit accrues to child and man; it is an experience having the most beneficent consequences upon the pursuit of happiness. For Wordsworth is a practical humanist, an anthropocentrist in the long run, and it is his idea that we win our individual happiness not by challenging the opposing natural element but by embracing it. If we can obtain the sense of community with the infinite concretion of the environing world, we may cease to feel like small aliens, even though busy, cunning, and predatory ones. In our cultural paradigms we have a saying about the peace which passeth understanding, and one about the security of that perfect love which casteth out fear; and Wordsworth had deeply assimilated these biblical phrases. Such values, if we accept them, must be of even greater moment to us today than in the time of Wordsworth, in the degree of our increased alienation from nature and, I think, our increased anxiety. I shall assume that as Wordsworthians we are able to verify them in our own experience.

Wordsworth meant always to display the affections in their purest or most elemental form; therefore to treat the affections as they fixed themselves upon nature, and nature in her wild or original state, such as that of his Cumberland region—an advantage incidentally that most of his readers in their daily lives can never match. If our experience of nature is confined to enjoying the suburban lawn or garden, or the public park landscaped for the edification of our modern societies, there is always the possibility that a narcissistic element may creep into the experience and restrict it: we may be admiring man more than nature. And our occasional jolly picnics into the heart of nature somewhere may not take us decisively out of the consciousness of our confederated kind, and certainly do not give us time to develop the required feelings. Perhaps when we theorize about the great passions we will remark that it is possible for the boy or the man to fix his affections upon his human mother, but possible also in some sense to fix them upon the elemental mother who is nature. That would be an experience of ontological dignity. In the instructive mythology of Freud we learn a great deal about the one mother, but nothing about the other. But let me offer a modern or post-Wordsworthian fable. Its parts may be found, though isolated and not much developed, in John Dewey's writings, for example. There was a time when man with his principle of individuation had not emerged from the matrix, the maternal womb, of nature, nor had his problems emerged with him. But in due time he was brought forth, the umbilical cord was severed. Then began that long torture in which he now throve upon his aggressions, and now stood fixed in guilt and fear, toward that nature who no longer contained him but indifferently confronted him; the subjective-objective duality so bitterly felt in our modern philosophers. Very well. But the fable says that man nevertheless discovered in himself a wonderful gift for what is called "aesthetic" experience; and that in this aesthetic experience the hateful distinction between subject and object is for once obliterated. In this experience man returns to nature, his mother, yet in his own character, and without suffering death. This is fable or myth. The first part, about man's birth out of nature, is evidently suggested by the hypothesis of biological evolution; the second part, about his salvation, goes back most directly to the idealistic German philosophers. This second part would have made quick sense to Wordsworth. He possessed the principle of it through the conversations with Coleridge, at the time when their friendship was perfect, when each required the other to give his whole thought, and the other withheld nothing.

We think of *The Prelude* as the sequential account of scores of occasions where some given natural concretion presents itself to the boy and elicits his response. Nature is not offered by the poet, and could not be offered, in the visual fullness which is recorded by the painter. The concretion tends to be massive yet individualized, and its presence is likely to enter unexpectedly and dramatically into the consciousness of a boy who is about the business of a boy. The response of the boy's feelings will generally persuade us; it is good drama, and we have been boys.

But I am afraid we have to consider something in the response of that boy after all which we feel like resisting, or more probably feel like reading very carelessly or even skipping in order not to resist. A heavy overlay of religious experience is added to the spontaneous joy of the boy's simple affections. A more or less uniform religious doctrine is adhered to throughout the poem, and brought to consciousness within the boy's response almost every time before the poet will leave him alone. (And of course there are the systematic doctrinal meditations interpolated at many places by the poet himself.) The doctrine has been studied by many scholars. Here is probably the hardest as well as the last understanding of Wordsworth which they have had to master.

It is a doctrine of pantheism, or natural religion, or pan-psychism, or Behmenism; Professor Stallknecht shows conclusively, so far as I am concerned, how closely at many points Wordsworth follows the teachings of Jacob Boehme.[3] Of course he follows others of similar teaching, and with all his eclecticism may still at many places put the doctrine in his own words. But as I understand it, by the least statement of this religion of nature we must conceive the boy's experience under color of the following beliefs: (a) that the spirit of the natural universe focusses all its terrific power in the given concretion; and (b) that this is expressly for the purpose of aggressively seeking him out and making itself known to him and giving him its joy. I say "it" rather than "he" for the sake of keeping to Wordsworth's thought. This is according to a theory of religion which is on the order of his theory of the poetic diction: an experience that sticks close to its tenor, while that tenor consists in the pure natural concretions, and does not intend to offer the presence under the figure of "personifications," which would convert it into a human image and perpetrate the pathetic fallacy. How can he avoid it? Now I should not wish to scorn a cosmic compassion which resorts by such tricks, such very human tricks, to these philanthropic aggressions.

[3] *Strange Seas of Thought*, Durham, 1945.

But in the name of David Hartley, who is another of Wordsworth's heroes, I suggest that pragmatically, psychologically, it is more usual for us to regard the cosmic constructs of religion as fashioned afterwards, and indeed upon the base of those spontaneous affective responses which people make to nature; so that in the ordering which Wordsworth authorizes, the cart is before the horse. We have a mystical experience which precedes its own empirical technique. The independent lyrics of Wordsworth are not burdened with all this significance, and those readers who do not know *The Prelude* can think of him as a lyric poet who is content on the whole with his *métier*. Of course the early appearance of *Tintern Abbey* may startle them, for that was the prelude to *The Prelude*. I think they may respond to it by regarding its eloquence as that of a kind of straining, muddled Protestant theologism; for so William Empson regarded it; he was not aware that its terms were those of an already stated theology, and perhaps regular enough in that kind of orthodoxy. *The Prelude* is a religious poem, and unquestionably means much to many Wordsworthians in that sense. Even so, we cannot but wonder if he does not read back into the boy's mind some of the matured configurations of his own. And I think we may prefer to take our poetry as an experience which is local, and plural, rather than cosmic, and one. It will still give the quick joy, and the instant sense of community with the natural objects, and we can go a long way on that.

For me the important successors to Wordsworth in the poetry of nature have been Keats, and Hopkins, and our own Robert Frost. Of these Hopkins is the only analogue of the Wordsworth of *The Prelude*; Hopkins subsumed the love of nature under a religious dispensation. But Hopkins was a Roman, and even the militant order of the Society of Jesus was a comfortable dispensation which, so to speak, laid down once for all the stipulations of an all-embracing faith, and did not mean that afterwards the common believer should compel every spontaneous experience to disclose its dogmatic bearings. The doctrine of Scotus gave to Hopkins his special charter. It allowed him to seek the "dapple" in things, where we are challenged by a natural effect that surely cannot be contained by the intellect. In the poem *Pied Beauty* this priest is uninhibited in his presentation of the humblest natural beauty. He crosses himself at the beginning, as it were, where he says, "Glory be to God for dappled things"; and at the end, where he ascribes this beauty to God's creation though God's own beauty is past dapple and change. I think this must be the version of religious nature-poetry which in our literature is the classical one. The believer has embraced the faith, attended his masses, performed his tithes; it is assumed that his spontaneous activities now will not have to be too careful doctrinally. Including his making of verses, and even making them about nature, if that is one of them; the father confessor will neither question their innocence, nor induce a fatal self-consciousness in the poet by showing him how they lead the philosophic mind toward God. There is no indication that Hopkins' superiors offered any reproach against his *Wreck of the Deutschland,* where he permitted himself to lay a daring interpretation upon the action of the tall nun who called out from the deck of the foundering ship to Christ to "Come quickly." Was she asking Christ to give her crown to her now, and to let it be though in heaven just the familiar landscape of springtime in place of those winter seas? Already she can sense the dreadful fog lifting:

> For how to the heart's cheering
> The down-dugged ground-hugged grey
> Hovers off, the jay-blue heavens appearing
> Of pied and peeled May!

But of course the fertile Hopkins can think of other interpretations for her cry, all of them more orthodox. Death is after all an official occasion for the priest. Let us hope that dogma will keep its dignity upon that tempting and infinitely delicate occasion.

I am ignorant in these matters. But I should like in the concluding note to offer the speculation that Wordsworth himself may have repented of the dogmatic zeal of his *Prelude,* or at any rate allowed it to worry him endlessly. The evidence is chiefly in the *Ode on Intimations of Immortality,* that poem of Wordsworth's which beyond all the others is splendid, beyond them confused in its argument, and destined to be mooted.

Wordsworth has told us that the first four stanzas of the *Ode* were composed at one time (and it was while the composition of *The Prelude* was under way), but that a period of several years intervened before the other seven stanzas were added (by which time of course *The Prelude* had been finished and laid away till its author could make up his mind to publish it). In the early part of the *Ode* the speaker mourns because nature does not now wear for him the celestial light, the glory, in which it was once arrayed. It still has its loveliness. A certain personal episode is mentioned in the third stanza:

> Now, while the birds thus sing a joyous song,
> And while the young lambs bound
> As to the tabor's sound,
> To me alone there came a thought of grief:
> A timely utterance gave that thought relief,
> And I again am strong.

What was the timely utterance? Professor Trilling suggests that it was *Resolution and Independence,* the poem about the aged leech gatherer composed near this time.[4] But the trouble which is healed by the meeting with the leech gatherer can hardly be the trouble which is the burden of the *Ode.* In the pertinent part of the smaller poem we read:

> I heard the sky-lark warbling in the sky;
> And I bethought me of the playful hare:

---

[4] *The Liberal Imagination,* New York, 1950, 138-41.

> Even such a happy Child of earth am I;
> Even as these blissful creatures do I fare;
> Far from the world I walk, and from all care;
> But there may come another day to me—
> Solitude, pain of heart, distress, and poverty.

He goes on to wonder how he can expect others to provide for his livelihood, and the thought of Chatterton and Burns reminds him how poets "begin in gladness; But thereof come in the end despondency and madness." Then as if providentially he meets the leech gatherer, who is decrepit and poverty-stricken but has no fear, and he is comforted. The animal or economic discouragement represented here is unusual with Wordsworth, whether in his poems or in his life so far as we have it. The Wordsworth of our impression is about as tough as a leech gatherer. We are tempted to think he offers himself in this weakness mostly in order to make a dramatic foil to the leech gatherer. But this assumption is not necessary. What we are sure of is that the mood would not fit the *Ode*, where the poet's complaint is that he no longer obtains from natural objects the religious intimations which he ascribes to his youth; that is to say, the overwhelming sense of the presence of God. So I prefer to follow the usual opinion which identifies the "timely utterance" with the little poem, *My heart leaps up when I behold*. The last lines of this poem are placed by the poet under the title of the *Ode* as a text, and the complete poem is as follows:

> My heart leaps up when I behold
>   A rainbow in the sky:
> So was it when my life began;
> So is it now I am a man;
> So be it when I shall grow old,
>   Or let me die!
> The Child is father of the Man;

And I could wish my days to be
Bound each to each by natural piety.

For me this perfect little poem seems to say by indirection that the important thing in the child's experience was the spontaneous joy of seeing the rainbow; and the full sense of God which belongs to the man with his laborious dogma may not really have been there. The joy was enough, and it is enough now if the man has never lost the gift for joy. The idea of the "natural piety" is not according to Boehme, I believe, but quite according to Hartley, ancestor perhaps of our contemporary psychology with its habit of associations and derivations. Parenthetically, however, we do have to notice that the locution itself is somewhat foreign to our psychological jargon. To know what piety is we have to have read Virgil and seen how Aeneas was pious because he honored his father Anchises, and bore him upon his own back from burning Troy. That was a piety symbolic of how each day a man must take up the life of yesterday, so that no human gift or possession will be allowed to fail.

The gift for responding to the rainbow had not failed for Wordsworth. But at the end of stanza four he is still troubled: the fact remains in spite of the "timely utterance" that he cannot instantly read from his present experience what his big work has been so confidently attributing to the youthful experience. He tests it in laboratory fashion by crucial experiments, with a tree, a field, and a pansy:

Oh evil day! if I were sullen
While Earth herself is adorning,
This sweet May-morning,
And the Children are culling
On every side,
In a thousand valleys far and wide,
Fresh flowers; while the sun shines warm,
And the Babe leaps up on his Mother's arm:—

110

I hear, I hear, with joy I hear!
—But there's a Tree, of many, one,
A single Field which I have looked upon,
Both of them speak of something that is gone:
　　The Pansy at my feet
　　Doth the same tale repeat:
Whither is fled the visionary gleam?
Where is it now, the glory and the dream?

We gather that he is not yet prepared to fall back upon the satisfactions of natural piety. He will let the poem wait in order to see if he can recover the visionary gleam.

In the long concluding part of the *Ode* he tries a desperate dogmatic expedient. He compounds his dogmas now; or perhaps he waives the old one while he tries the new one. The new one is the Platonic dogma of recollection, whereby the freshly incarnated soul of the child recalls its pre-migrationary dignities. Perhaps the religious overtones of the child's vision as Wordsworth thinks of them can be accounted for more simply in that way. But he is honest enough to indicate in his preface to the finished poem that this dogma is not particularly congenial to him, and that a religious system will scarcely find in it a very firm support. And in the latter stanzas the man is no more able than before to have the experience which he imputes to the child. He still wavers between mourning for his disability and making the most of the natural piety. For his conclusion it is practically as well as artistically needful for him to be content with what he has. He concludes quietly:

To me the meanest flower that blows can give
Thoughts that do often lie too deep for tears.

I believe this means that the flower addresses him as a lyrical object, and that he can then *think* himself into full religious consciousness very much as a priest will turn any spontaneous experience by his dialectic into occasion for glorifying God. But this is a process of intellect not given in the original in-

111

tuition. The idea that the child saw God in the flower surely and intuitively is the ground on which Wordsworth has pronounced him "Mighty Prophet," "Seer blest," and "best Philosopher." But in that case the man has simply not inherited fully from the child's estate. Natural piety has not worked.

The concern which Wordsworth registers in the *Ode* will perhaps have for us not only its face value there, but another which we can infer: a disillusionment with the achievement of the great *Prelude*. In that poem he has read off to his adult readers the intuitive religiousness of the child as if it were a universal and exemplary experience. But what if the adult mind cannot have this experience? Wordsworth came to the melancholy conviction that it lacked the power. And what if the child's mind lacked it too, if Wordsworth in the excess of his prodigious memory had given it more power than it had had? I think we will imagine that this question harrowed the poet.

What we do know is that Wordsworth did not take pleasure in the completed *Prelude*, with all its magnificence, and the sense of its having taken the best labors of his life. While he was writing it, his intimates and he spoke of it as part of the broad philosophical project, *The Recluse*, as Professor Garrod has shown. But he published the middle third part of *The Recluse* in 1814, under the title *The Excursion*; and in its preface he referred to another work, evidently *The Prelude*, as only "preparatory," and concerned with the author's development and credentials as a poet and philosopher. Even so, he withheld its publication, and that came about only after his death, and the title as we have it was supplied by his widow.

What we lose by finding this significance in the *Ode*, and in *The Prelude* in the light of the *Ode*, is a certain epistemology, or psychology, of the religious experience. A man does not seem to have a complete version of it in the intuitive manner with which Wordsworth endowed the child. And perhaps the child did not really have it that way, either. But what we are left with is a very full account of Wordsworth's religious experience itself at a certain period, however it may have been achieved; and what seems even more essential, because it would be the condition of a religious experience, always the spontaneous and lyrical joy in nature which is aesthetic experience. The short poems which Wordsworth wrote are rarely affected by our present discussion. He referred to them as the "little cells, oratories, and sepulchral recesses" which flowered out from the sacred "edifice" of his intended great poem. But the figure is misleading. They are the fundamental earth, or they are the foundation stones, upon which if there is to be a religious edifice it must rise.

WORDSWORTH
AND THE EUROPEAN PROBLEM OF THE
TWENTIETH CENTURY

BY B. IFOR EVANS

May I begin with a personal note? It was in the United States, in Iowa City, in 1925 that I first heard the name of Professor George McLean Harper and of his study of the life, works, and influence of William Wordsworth.[1] I suppose that reflects somewhat on my education. It also reflects upon that European view which I hope to develop in this chapter. The Preface to Harper's great work was dated from Princeton on July 9, 1915, a month and a year when I was still a schoolboy and when England was beginning to realize the cruel pressure of the first of two world wars. I ought to have read "Harper" sometime during the next decade, but it is strange, if we are honest with ourselves, to realize how many great and memorable books we fail to read. I had been lecturing upon literature for four years by 1925. I had even lectured on Wordsworth, but I was still ignorant of this great study which was then and still remains today at the center of Wordsworth studies. So it was only when in Iowa City in 1925 after one of my young and immature discourses that, faced with a student who asked me if I had read "Harper," I went to the library and read the first edition of this work, which, surely, in some ways we are commemorating, along with the poet who was its theme.

Much of its greatness lay in the desire of one who was so obviously genuine and fair in his own nature to carry those virtues into his studies. After all, Harper, if some allowance is made for the style and manner of his period, is still of all the critics the one who gives the most balanced portrait. There

[1] New York and London, 2 vols., 1916.

114

are the radicals who exploit the theory of the "lost leader"; there are those who elevate Wordsworth's love for Annette Vallon, and the birth of a daughter outside wedlock, into a unique incident in Anglo-French relations; and there is Dr. Edith Batho in her brave and learned book, *The Later Wordsworth,* becoming a special pleader in her attempt to answer the more adverse criticisms. Harper had, of course, an idealism which may seem a little naïve in a world overshadowed by cruel, materialistic, and savage values which he could never have understood, but it remains a life which I think Wordsworth himself would have appreciated.

Professor Harper had, also, a moment of direct contact with the event which we commemorate today. "I have heard," he wrote, "from the lips of one of the few persons now living who knew him, Miss Arnold, of Fox How, an account of that morning. 'My younger sister and I,' she said, 'went up on the terrace of Loughrigg, and watched the windows of Rydal Mount opposite; and when the curtains were drawn down we knew Wordsworth was dead.' "[2]

Before dealing with Wordsworth and our contemporary European problem I should like to comment on the controversy which his work has aroused and its relation to his poetical achievement. He was himself partly responsible for the misinterpretations to which he has been subjected. He tried to persuade himself, and to persuade others, that his poetry was based on a theory. He was led to this partly by a bold independence of mind which developed at times even to arrogance, and partly because at the most formative period of his life as a poet Coleridge was ever close at hand. In the early days Wordsworth's views on poetry were affected by that radical element which was present in him, though it never dominated his whole nature, and the radical element gave him a certain pleasure in stating views that he knew would surprise, disturb, and even shock. It was from some such background

[2] *William Wordsworth,* II, 436.

that he was led with Coleridge in the Advertisement to the first edition of *Lyrical Ballads* to say that the poems were written "chiefly with a view to ascertain how far the language of conversation in the middle and lower classes of society is adapted to the purposes of poetic pleasure."

Wordsworth succeeds at his best as a poet when he has set aside theory and when he is using all the resources of his poetical strength, with much incidentally derived from earlier poets, and employing these resources to define his own experience or vision, particularly his vision arising out of experience. In the same way I think there is a danger in accepting Wordsworth too much at his own valuation as a constructive thinker, for although there is much that is incidentally valuable in his thought and at times there is great wisdom, there is nothing in his thought that matches the uniqueness of his approach towards experience or his vision. He is not very successful, unlike Coleridge or Keats, in describing in prose the nature of his best achievement as a poet, mainly because his most individual achievement is founded on intuition or vision. Strangely enough, one of his best attempts comes at the age of seventy-five after a talk with Tennyson: "You will be pleased to hear that he [Tennyson] expressed in the strongest terms his gratitude to my writings. To this I was far from indifferent, though persuaded that he is not much in sympathy with what I should myself most value in my attempts; namely, the spirituality with which I have endeavored to invest the material Universe, and the moral relation under which I have wished to exhibit its most ordinary appearances."[3]

If what is best in Wordsworth goes outside systematic thought, Coleridge on the other hand was a philosopher most industrious in his thought, despite what the critics may have said about his alleged opium-ridden indolence, a philosopher whose greatness and originality have been fully realized only

[3] Letter to Henry Reed, July 1, 1845. *Wordsworth and Reed,* ed. by L. N. Broughton, Ithaca, N.Y., 1933, 144.

in the twentieth century. But he was a philosopher who could not turn his philosophy into poetry. This is what he wished to do. This is what he often believed that Wordsworth was doing, and part of his great admiration for Wordsworth lies in his belief that Wordsworth was able to achieve something which he could not accomplish himself. When Coleridge abandoned systematic thought he went into some dream magic such as *The Ancient Mariner* or *Christabel.* Wordsworth, on those great occasions when he abandoned systematic thought, grew into a vision, and by vision I mean *Tintern Abbey* and the greatest passages of *The Prelude.*

These distinctions are necessary if a proper tribute is to be paid to the best in Wordsworth's poetry and if one is to understand the difference of order between a poem such as *The Ancient Mariner* and a poem such as *Tintern Abbey.* For *The Ancient Mariner* does not belong to the order of the greatest poetry. It lacks high seriousness. It is magic, not an interpretation of life. Reduce it to the terms of life and you reduce it to a tale with a moral ending. But *Tintern Abbey* is an interpretation of life through experience, not ordinary experience, but vision. This strange and powerful union of experience to vision, of an empirical mysticism, is a quality which Wordsworth possessed in a way different from any other English poet.

> A slumber did my spirit seal;
>   I had no human fears:
> She seemed a thing that could not feel
>   The touch of earthly years.
>
> No motion has she now, no force;
>   She neither hears nor sees;
> Rolled round in earth's diurnal course,
>   With rocks, and stones, and trees.

No trace of the vocabulary to which Wordsworth's theories

would lead, no philosophy, and yet a vision of life concentrated in eight miraculous lines.

Coleridge knew that when imagination took possession of him reason and philosophy departed. He knew that when he tried to translate consecutive thought into poetry he failed. He knew that his own experience could not become possessed of the imagination as in Wordsworth and reveal a new order of understanding. I have in my possession the copy of *Fears in Solitude* in which Coleridge wrote against the passage beginning "We have been too long Dupes of a deep delusion": "all the Lines so marked convey according to my conscience sound good sense; but unfortunately they are neither poetry, nor anything—as eloquence for instance which approximates to it. They are *Prose* that in a frolic has put on a masquerade dress of metre, and like most Masquerades, blundered in the assumed character."

Because Wordsworth had this unique quality of vision arising from experience, I would submit that an excessive importance has been attached to other elements in his thought and work, many of which are commonplace. Thus, for instance, I would maintain that as far as political thought is concerned Wordsworth is less original, one might even venture to add less important than some of his critics have thought. His early enthusiasm for the French Revolution was based partly upon the radicalism of youth and a reading of Rousseau and on an admiration for the peasants of his native dales. It is the same sort of radicalism that had a later poetical manifestation in the Advertisement to *Lyrical Ballads*. It had further a basis in experience, for Wordsworth had seen the life of the French peasants of which there are moving descriptions in *The Prelude*, and had felt that it was necessary to bring this tyranny and serfdom to an end. So he describes how when he was walking with Beaupuy he met

a hunger-bitten girl,
Who crept along fitting her languid gait

118

Unto a heifer's motion, by a cord
Tied to her arm, and picking thus from the lane
Its sustenance, while the girl with pallid hands
Was busy knitting in a heartless mood
Of solitude, and at the sight my friend
In agitation said, " 'Tis against *that*
That we are fighting."[4]

In his mind there was a contrast between the life of the French peasant and the sturdy independence and freedom which he saw, or thought he saw, in his own native valleys.

This was followed by a sentiment which is common enough as the aftermath of a revolutionary period: a hatred and fear of the dictator or man of power who emerges triumphant from a revolution. Wordsworth in his complex thoughts about Napoleon finds fear dominant with some sort of emotion near to dread and admiration at the same time. This can be found in the Rob Roy poem—its mood must not be treated with complete seriousness, but when Wordsworth is speaking of Rob Roy he is thinking of Napoleon.

That dread of the tyrant, that desire for order, led Wordsworth to the beginning of a more conservative approach to life, and one need not be surprised unless one has imagined the early political thought as being original, or unless one has felt that the best of the poetry was somehow dependent upon political thinking, or indeed unless one had that other heresy that only radicals can write verse.

During a period when he was still at the height of his poetical powers, however, there did come into Wordsworth's life an influence which led him to think far better of the aristocratic, titled and, above all, landowning classes than he had at any previous period of his career. I am surprised to see how many works on Wordsworth deal only incidentally with Sir George Beaumont, for Beaumont was an important formative

[4] *The Prelude* (1850), IX, 510-18.

influence. I can point to very reputable works which fail to mention Sir George once in the whole course of their narrative. It is interesting to record that Professor Harper, thorough in this as in so many other matters, rightly assumed on the basis of less information than is now available the importance of Sir George Beaumont's influence: "A new current," he wrote, "had begun to flow into Wordsworth's life shortly before he set out on the Scottish tour. It was an influence destined to alter profoundly his character and his art. That the acceptance of patronage affects the relation of the recipient to his benefactor is a rule of nature. The utmost delicacy of the giver and the proudest independence of the receiver never suffice to annul it altogether. . . . No poet could have wished for a more high-minded patron than Sir George Beaumont. It was natural for a man of his great wealth to think that Wordsworth's narrow means were poverty, and that he might achieve more if relieved from the necessity of rigorous thrift. His benefactions were not alarmingly large, and no doubt they were not only prompted by genuine kindness, but proffered most delicately. He was himself a fellow-artist, and there were abundant grounds for the friendship that sprang up between him and Wordsworth. Nevertheless, in Wordsworth's letters to him there is perceptible an effort to adapt himself to a new point of view. To most of his correspondents Wordsworth had been stiffly uncompromising. He wrote few letters, and in them there was usually a touch of almost rude independence. One would suppose from his long and frequent epistles to Sir George that at last he acknowledged a superior. Of course, it is not to be imagined that Wordsworth surrendered a particle of his self-respect. But that his attitude towards society was modified by this new relationship there can be scarcely any doubt, and in the end his art reflected the change."[5] I would qualify this comment which I have not quoted in full only by adding that to my mind the relation had a more intimate basis

[5] *William Wordsworth*, II, 68-9.

in friendship than Professor Harper suggests. In years when the public was treating him very harshly, Wordsworth found in Sir George Beaumont one who not only wished to extend towards him a genial hand of patronage, but who with his wife appreciated his work.

Sir George was after all himself an artist, even if not a very good one. His collection of masterpieces of painting included not only the great classical works, but examples of contemporaries whom he cherished. I have a collection of the letters that James Wilkie, who painted *The Blind Fiddler*, had written to him. They are not the letters of the patronized to the patron; they are exchanges between two equals. Beaumont's collection of paintings was so important, and his sense of public duty so great, that his gift of them to the nation led to the founding of the National Gallery in London. Beaumont was also deeply interested in the picturesque, in the relationship of one's house and estate to their natural surroundings. I have a long series of letters which Uvedale Price wrote him on these matters. With Beaumont's influence Wordsworth began to see the influence of the planned scene and the aesthetic pleasure it gave, rather than the sudden profound experience, spiritual in quality, gained, as so often in his early poetry, from a scene whose elements were ordinary.

One cannot understand Wordsworth's violent reaction to the Reform Bill unless one understands all that Sir George Beaumont represented in his mind. For to Wordsworth the Reform Bill meant handing political power to the new manufacturers, and the new manufacturers were those who would come with their railways, with their factories, and with all that destroyed nature in the forms in which Wordsworth admired it, to the more delectable parts of England, even to the Lake District itself. Sir George represented the landowner who was a man of taste, who would preserve the countryside, who knew his tenantry, who loved artists, bought their pictures, and encouraged them to continue writing their poems. There is of course more in it than this, but I am convinced that despite Wordsworth's violence of comment his central fear of the Reform Bill was an intelligible one and not based, as some of his critics have suggested, upon a wild prejudice.

There remains the problem of whether Sir George's influence was a desirable one, and here I think one approaches a very complex question. Sir George was the patron at his best, never interfering, always encouraging, and with a wife who seemed to have a most kindly nature and a real understanding of verse. Yet the problems of landscape gardening in Sir George's home at Coleorton, the attachment to the picturesque, all led Wordsworth to become more interested in the beauties of nature than in that mystical experience arising from commonplace, even homely scenes, which had governed him in his most creative years. For behind *Tintern Abbey* and *The Prelude* there is not the beauty of the individual scene but a high and unique experience arising often from the very simplest elements. I would therefore suggest that it is very probable that, unwittingly, Sir George's influence helped to confuse in Wordsworth's mind the difference between his unique vision and mere descriptive nature poetry. So it might be said that apart from all questions of diminution of poetic power Sir George is partly responsible for the difference of point of view in the nature descriptions of *The Prelude* and *The Excursion*. On the other hand it would, I think, be a respectable view that what was unique in Wordsworth was in any case dimming and disappearing, at least after the end of the first few years of his acquaintance with Sir George and Lady Beaumont.

I am therefore arguing in the first place that much in Wordsworth's thought is of a far more ordinary character than is usually believed. His contribution to thought, to philosophy, and to literary criticism is not new and illuminating and profound as is that of Coleridge. Secondly, that while much in Wordsworth's verses reaches very high ranges of accomplishment, his true greatness lies in a uniqueness of experience to be found in *Tintern Abbey* and parts of *The Prelude* and in some other places. When he reaches this order of writing he achieves something greater than the political sonnets or the *Ode to Duty*, whose methods and achievement can ultimately be analyzed. In these other and most original poems, a new humanism is made out of his faith that man, through the definition of his own experience in his relationships with nature, can confirm in himself the life of the spirit.

I would thus define my position in relationship to Wordsworth before attempting to explore his importance for what I have called, in general terms, "the European problem of the twentieth century."

In one way it could be urged that Wordsworth's poetry had worked against one of the most urgent needs of the modern age. For the major problem of this modern period has been to discover how civilization can be maintained by a large and overcrowded urban population. Wordsworth had seen the danger of these modern industrial conditions. He describes the "increasing accumulation of men in cities, where the uniformity of their occupations produces a craving for extraordinary incident."[6] But his art implies that lakes, mountains, loneliness, and the rural scene generally were the necessary background for poetry. In London, in the "monstrous ant-hill on the plain," poetry was impossible. Charles Lamb tried jokingly to contradict this view, but the matter cannot be settled in his light-hearted terms. For the majority of men and women have to live in towns, whether they wish to or not. If they are to have beauty it must be discovered in urban conditions. If verse, through the service of the imagination, is to inform them of much that is otherwise imperceptible in their experience, it must be by reference to urban ways of life.

Wordsworth, it is true, saw the danger. He saw that modern men and women would work in ugly and untidy towns and

[6] Preface to the second edition of *Lyrical Ballads*.

123

take their pleasures and consolations in the country. When he was opposing the extension of the railway into the Lake District, one of the arguments he had to meet was that it would be very educational for the inhabitants of the great manufacturing towns of Lancashire to see the Lakes. He was against "packing off men after this fashion, for holiday entertainment." Let the "master-manufacturers" instead "consent to a Ten Hours' Bill, with little, or, if possible, no diminution of wages, and the necessaries of life being more easily procured, the mind will develop itself accordingly, and each individual would be more at liberty to make, at his own cost, excursions in any direction which might be most inviting to him. There would then be no need for their masters sending them in droves scores of miles from their homes and families to the borders of Windermere, or anywhere else."[7] Yet while Wordsworth saw the problem, his poetry helped to make nature superlatively the poetical theme and urban civilization a helpless untidiness and weariness of the spirit. One can see it all working out later when the Knights in Tennyson's *Idylls* seem to move up and down England carefully avoiding the industrial towns. The great illusion of the nineteenth century is that it will ultimately be able to get back to the country. Its whole poetic tradition was linked with a rural romanticism. It never attempted to plan the town, the mining village, the industrial center. There lay the tragedy of England's nineteenth-century industrialism, as anyone can see even today in England.

Wordsworth lived in one industrial revolution as we in another. He was aware of the problem of his age, but in a way he retired from it. Could Wordsworth and the other romantic writers have achieved something with town civilization had they attempted it? Could they have broken down that separateness between the artist and the community which is part of the problem of our time? The faith of the greatest artist should be, I suppose, to create beauty where now there is chaos

[7] *The Later Wordsworth*, by E. C. Batho, Cambridge, 1933, 207.

and ugliness. The modern artist can tell us of the chaos and ugliness without helping us to remove them. Wordsworth had ultimately this degree of egoism: that he put himself before society. I know that what I am suggesting is impossible, for the artist cannot thus control his imagination to a prescribed social purpose. If Wordsworth had lived in the cities he might have written as he could do at his worst. As it is, his release to nature gave him an exaltation which he has carried over to thousands of others:

> it is shaken off,
> As by miraculous gift 'tis shaken off,
> That burthen of my own unnatural self,
> . . . whither shall I turn
> By road or pathway or through open field,
> Or shall a twig or any floating thing
> Upon the river, point me out my course?
> Enough that I am free; for months to come
> May dedicate myself to chosen tasks.[8]

I have already referred to those who attack Wordsworth violently for his alleged political apostasy and those who defend him without reserve. There is surely no need to maintain either position, for we in our age have experienced the very dilemma under which Wordsworth suffered. We have all known that promise of a new dawn, that faith that the early twentieth century had in itself, and which Wordsworth found in the French Revolution:

> a spirit was abroad
> Which could not be withstood, that poverty
> At least like this, would in a little time
> Be found no more, that we should see the earth
> Unthwarted in her wish to recompense
> The industrious, and the lowly Child of Toil,
> All institutes for ever blotted out

[8] *The Prelude* (1805-6), I, 21-34.

> That legalised exclusion, empty pomp
> Abolish'd, sensual state and cruel power
> Whether by edict of the one or few,
> And finally, as sum and crown of all,
> Should see the People having a strong hand
> In making their own Laws, whence better days
> To all mankind.[9]

It is very much as H. G. Wells used to write in his early and optimistic manner of the scientific utopias that lay ahead of us. Experience proved to our generation, as it did to Wordsworth, that evil is more dynamic and irradicable and the way harder than was once conceived. His own experience, especially in relation to the Reform Bill of 1832, marks out the other danger, the stiffening in reactionary opinion until the reason is dimmed. Wordsworth, as Dr. Batho shows, had some good reasons for opposing the Reform Bill, and she quotes some respectable opinions in support, both contemporary and later. But she fails to remove from my mind the impression of the violence with which Wordsworth expressed those views. I have already tried to show how, under the influence of Sir George Beaumont, he had come to feel that there was much to be said for the great landlords. He also foresaw some of the dangers of attempting to substitute a moderate reform of the franchise for more genuinely needed economic reforms. But what can explain the violence?

There are repercussions of it in a letter from Mrs. Wordsworth to Lady Beaumont of March 5, 1832; it is, I think, a letter previously unpublished. It will be recalled that there were rumors of cholera during that autumn of 1831 and the spring of 1832. Mrs. Wordsworth comments: "The Cholera *is* indeed a perplexing subject, but the thought disturbs us less than that of Reform." Those phrases are illuminating of the atmosphere of the Wordsworth household during those

[9] *Ibid.*, IX, 519-32.

126

months. They are the dread warning that in moving over from views which are radical or liberal or revolutionary, to the side that is cautious, calculating, and conservative, one should not move over to an atmosphere of unreasoning violence or prejudice, to the witch hunt instead of the argument, and that one should above all not deny the shape, the symbolic shape as it were, of one's own time.

There remains one matter compared with which all else is of minor importance. I have made reference to it once or twice in this chapter. It is that Wordsworth did at times reach an order of mystical vision in poetry which is of a quality without parallel in our literature, which cannot be explained in reference to psychology or philosophy, and which makes all his views on politics comparatively unimportant. I hesitate to quote the passages, for they have been so often repeated that their extraordinary quality is in danger of being obscured by excessive familiarity. Let me, however, venture to quote two passages. The first is interesting as it shows how that mystical vision in Wordsworth arises out of commonplace experience:

> The old Man still stood talking by my side;
> But now his voice to me was like a stream
> Scarce heard; nor word from word could I divide;
> And the whole body of the Man did seem
> Like one whom I had met with in a dream;
> Or like a man from some far region sent,
> To give me human strength, by apt admonishment.

> My former thoughts returned: the fear that kills;
> And hope that is unwilling to be fed;
> Cold, pain, and labour, and all fleshly ills;
> And mighty Poets in their misery dead.
> —Perplexed, and longing to be comforted,
> My question eagerly did I renew,
> "How is it that you live, and what is it you do?"

He with a smile did then his words repeat;
And said that, gathering leeches, far and wide
He travelled; stirring thus about his feet
The waters of the pools where they abide.
"Once I could meet with them on every side;
But they have dwindled long by slow decay;
Yet still I persevere, and find them where I may."

While he was talking thus, the lonely place,
The old Man's shape, and speech—all troubled me:
In my mind's eye I seemed to see him pace
About the weary moors continually,
Wandering about alone and silently.
While I these thoughts within myself pursued,
He, having made a pause, the same discourse renewed.[10]

Then, and one cannot avoid it in this discussion, there is
Tintern Abbey:

                              that blessed mood
In which the burthen of the mystery,
In which the heavy and the weary weight
Of all this unintelligible world,
Is lightened:—that serene and blessed mood,
In which the affections gently lead us on,—
Until, the breath of this corporeal frame
And even the motion of our human blood
Almost suspended, we are laid asleep
In body, and become a living soul:
While with an eye made quiet by the power
Of harmony, and the deep power of joy,
We see into the life of things.

What importance for us has all this from that period nearly
a century and a half ago when it was first written? It is that
here, without dogmatism, based on direct personal experience,
is a mystical faith in life and in its unity. Nor can this be dis-

[10] *Resolution and Independence,* 106-33.

missed as unsound by argument, or philosophy. For Wordsworth is not relating an argument or using rhetoric to persuade.
He is announcing a discovery, a vision, and its reality is declared in the verse which gives it form. W. P. Ker has, what
seems to me, a revealing passage on this matter: "His poetical
thought is not the poetical verifying of philosophical ideas
conveyed to his mind in books; it is the interpretation of his
own experience. His Ideal or Poetical world is the real world
of ordinary life, but perceived by him, William Wordsworth,
at different stages, day after day, in various illuminating ways.
As he reflects on his own ways of seeing the world, *Tintern
Abbey*, the *Prelude*, he knows that his mind is transcendental;
that what he sees is a revelation. Possibly at times under the
metaphysical influence of Coleridge he may have been led to
describe his mode of vision in terms like those of the idealist
philosophers. But no one who attends to Wordsworth's poetry
can believe that anything like regular philosophy was at the
beginning of his ideas."[11]

In Europe in the last ten years there has been a greater destruction of things that are beautiful in architecture, painting,
statuary, indeed in objects of all the arts, than in any period of
recorded history. There is further the spiritual recession, arising from the recognition of an evil and a barbarism of which
forty years ago one might have thought civilized man incapable. As one looks back from the period of the First World
War so many acts of mass cruelty, so many deliberate attempts
to degrade our human nature live so vividly in our memories
that they stand between us and the pleasures that we can gain
by looking at pictures, or statues, or even in listening to music
and poetry.

It is here that the mystical affirmation of Wordsworth,
merely because it is experience and not argument, makes the
supreme contribution. Sir Kenneth Clark in his study, *Land-*

[11] *Form and Style in Poetry*, ed. by R. W. Chambers, London, 1928,
118-19.

scape into Art, has shown how very closely related the painter
Constable was to Wordsworth. Constable and Wordsworth
"were united by their rapture in all created things."[12] Constable
wrote of the river Stour: "The sound of water escaping from
mill-dams, willows, old rotten planks, slimy posts, and brick-
work, I love such things. These scenes made me a painter, and
I am grateful." Again Constable wrote, "I never saw an ugly
thing in my life."[13] Constable, of course, did not end in that
mood, but Wordsworth was faithful to it. It is something as
reassuring of our powers to enjoy as the concept of evil and the
tread of barbarism, which we have witnessed in our time, have
been destructive of these powers. Wordsworth's contribution
is relevant because he had been through this valley of the
shadow of spiritual despair, and he had found a new and sustaining experience:

> it is shaken off,
> As by miraculous gift 'tis shaken off.

Sir Kenneth Clark, in attempting to define this quality present in Wordsworth as in Constable, is led to a passage in Tra-
herne "often quoted but indestructible," and with that I will
conclude: "You never enjoy the world aright, till the sea itself
floweth in your veins, till you are clothed with the heavens,
and crowned with the stars . . . yet further, and you never
enjoy the world aright, till you so love the beauty of enjoying
it that you are covetous and earnest to persuade others to enjoy it."

[12] London, 1949, 79.   [13] *Ibid.*

WORDSWORTH
AND THE IRON TIME

BY LIONEL TRILLING

Tᴴɪꜱ symposium must inevitably be charged with the consciousness that if Wordsworth were not kept in mind by the universities, he would scarcely be remembered at all. In our culture it is not the common habit to read the books of a century ago, and very likely all that we can mean when we say that a writer of the past is "alive" in people's minds is that, to those who once read him as a college assignment or who have formed an image of him from what they have heard about him, he exists as an attractive idea, as an intellectual possibility. If we think of the three poets whom Matthew Arnold celebrated in his *Memorial Verses,* we know that Byron is still attractive and possible, and so is Goethe, as was indicated recently by the elaborateness with which the bicentenary of his birth was celebrated. But Wordsworth is not attractive and not an intellectual possibility. He was once the great, the speaking poet for all who read English. He spoke both to the ordinary reader and to the literary man. But now the literary man outside the university will scarcely think of referring to Wordsworth as an important event of modern literature; and to the ordinary reader he is likely to exist as the very type of the poet whom life has passed by, presumably for the very good reason that he passed life by.

The discrepancy between the opinion of the world and the opinion, or at least the pious action, of the universities is a matter which in itself is worthy of comment and I should like to touch upon certain of its implications. But my chief intention is to ask what are the reasons for the world's present opinion of Wordsworth and how far that opinion is justified. By trying to answer these questions I hope to arrive at an under-

131

standing of Wordsworth suitable for our time, and thus to praise him.

If we ask why Wordsworth is no longer the loved poet he once was, why, indeed, he is felt to be absurd and even a little despicable, one answer that suggests itself is that for modern taste he is too Christian a poet. He is certainly not to be wholly characterized by the Christian element of his poetry. Nor can we say of him that he is a Christian poet in the same sense that Dante is, or Donne, or Hopkins. With them the specific Christian feeling and doctrine is of the essence of their matter and conscious intention, as it is not with Wordsworth. Yet at the present time, the doctrinal tendency of the world at large being what it is, that which *is* Christian in Wordsworth may well seem to be more prominent than it ever was before, and more decisive. I have in mind his concern for the life of humbleness and quiet, his search for peace, his sense of the burdens of this life, those which are inherent in the flesh and spirit of man. Then there is his belief that the bonds of society ought to be inner and habitual, not merely external and formal, and that the strengthening of these bonds by the acts and attitudes of charity is a great and charming duty. Christian too seems his responsiveness to the idea that there is virtue in the discharge of duties that are not humble, those which are of the great world and therefore dangerous to simple peace. There is his impulse to submit to the conditions of life under a guidance which is at once certain and mysterious; his sense of the possibility and actuality of enlightenment, it need scarcely be said, is one of the characteristic things about him. It was not he who said that the world was a vale of soul-making, but the poet who did make this striking paraphrase of the Christian sentiment could not have uttered it had not Wordsworth made it possible for him to do so. And then above all, there is his consciousness of the *neighbor*, his impulse to bring into the circle of significant life those of the neighbors who are simple and outside the circle of social pride, and also those who, in the judgment of the world, are queer and strange and useless.

Certainly this which I have called Christian in Wordsworth scarcely approaches, let alone makes up, the sum of Christianity. But then no personal document or canon can do that, not even the work of a poet who is specifically Christian in the way of Dante, or of Donne, or of Hopkins. When we speak of a poet as being of a particular religion, we do not imply in him completeness or orthodoxy, or even explicitness of doctrine, but only that his secular utterance has the decisive mark of the religion upon it. And if a religion is manifold in its aspects and extensive in time, the marks that are to be found on the poets who are in a relation to it will be various in kind. It seems to me that the marks of Christianity on Wordsworth are clear and indelible. It is therefore worth trying the hypothesis that the world today does not like him because it does not like the Christian quality and virtues.

But the question at once arises whether this hypothesis is actually available to us. Professor Fairchild says, and in a very explicit way, that it is not. In the chapter on Wordsworth in the third volume of his *Religious Trends in English Poetry,* he not only says that Wordsworth is not a Christian poet but he also expresses doubts that Wordsworth was ever properly to be called a Christian, even when he became a communicant of the Church and its defender. He even goes so far as to tell us that as a poet Wordsworth is actually dangerous to the Christian faith. He is dangerous in the degree that he is religious at all, for his religion is said to be mere religiosity, the religion of nothing more than the religious emotion, beginning and ending in the mere sense of transcendence. Naked of dogma, bare of precise predication of God and the nature of man, this religiosity of Wordsworth's is to be understood as a pretentious and seductive rival of Christianity. It is the more dangerous because it gives license to man's pretensions—Professor Fairchild subscribes to the belief which is not uncom-

monly held by proponents of religion, or by those who defend
what they call a classical view of the world, that romanticism
must bear a large part of the responsibility for our present
ills, especially for those which involve man's direct and conscious inhumanity to man.

We can surely find a degree of cogency in Professor Fairchild's argument within the terms of its intention. The nineteenth century was in many respects a very Christian century,
but in the aspect of it which bulks largest in our minds it developed chiefly the ethical and social parts of Christian belief
and no doubt at the cost of the dogmatic part, which had
already been weakened by the latitudinarian tendency of the
eighteenth century. And it is probably true that when the
dogmatic principle in religion is slighted, religion goes along
for a while on generalized emotion and ethical intention—
"morality touched by emotion"—and then loses the force of its
impulse, even the essence of its being. In this sort of attenuation of religion, romanticism in general and Wordsworth in
particular did indeed play a great part by making the sense
of transcendence and immanence so real and so attractive.

It is certainly true that, through the most interesting and
creative part of his career, Wordsworth cut himself off from a
conscious involvement with or reference to the doctrinal teachings of the Church. He spoke of the virtues of faith, hope, and
charity without reference to the specifically Christian source
and end of these virtues. His sense of the need for salvation
did not, certainly, take account of the Christian means of salvation. Of evil in the Christian sense of the word, of sin as an
element of the nature of man, he also took no account. And yet,
all this being true, as we look at him in the context of his own
time and in the context of our own time, what may properly
be called his Christian element can be made to speak to us, as
it spoke to so many Christians in the nineteenth century, as it
spoke to so many who were not Christians and made them in
one degree or another accessible to Christianity.

"Any religious movement," says Christopher Dawson, an orthodox Christian scholar, "which adopts a purely critical and negative attitude to culture is . . . a force of destruction and disintegration which mobilizes against it the healthiest and most constructive elements in society—elements which can by no means be dismissed as worthless from the religious point of view."[1] Romanticism in general was far from worthless to Christianity, far from worthless to that very Anglo-Catholicism which likes to be so strict with it. And this is true of Wordsworth in particular. He certainly did not in his great period accept as adequate what the Church taught about the nature of man. But he was one of the few poets who really discovered something about the nature of man. And what he discovered can no doubt be shown, if the argument be conducted by a comparison of formulas and doctrine, to be at variance with the teachings of Christianity. Yet I think it can also be shown that he discovered much that a strong Christianity must take acount of, and be easy with, and make use of. It can be shown too that the Church, consciously or not, has found advantage in what Wordsworth told us of the nature of man.

Professor Fairchild understands Christianity far better than I do through having studied it ever so much more than I have; and of course he understands it far better than I might ever hope to because he has experienced it as a communicant. He has also, I am sure, tested his conclusions by the whole tendency of the Church to which he gives so strong and thoughtful an allegiance; my own reading of this tendency, at least as it appears in literature and in literary criticism where it has been so influential, is that it is not inclined to accept Wordsworth as a Christian poet. As against the force of Professor Fairchild's judgment, I cannot help feeling that there is an important element of Christianity with which Wordsworth has a significant affinity, even though this element is not now of

[1] *Religion and Culture*, London, 1948, 206.

a chief importance to Christian intellectuals. But this is not
an occasion for anything like contentiousness, and I ought
not to seem to be forcing even a great poet into a faith whose
members do not want him there. I am not, in any case, so much
concerned to prove that Wordsworth is a Christian poet as
to account for a certain quality in him which makes him unacceptable to the modern world. And so, without repudiating
my first hypothesis, I shall abandon it for this fresh one: that
the quality in Wordsworth that now makes him unacceptable
is a Judaic quality.

My knowledge of the Jewish tradition is, I fear, all too slight
to permit me to hope that I can develop this new hypothesis
in any very enlightening way. Yet there is one Jewish work of
traditional importance which I happen to know with some
intimacy and it lends a certain color of accuracy to my notion.
This is the work called *Pirke Aboth,* that is, the sayings, the
sententiae, of the Fathers. It was edited in the second century
of the present era by the scholar and teacher who bore the
magnificent name of Rabbi Jehudah the Prince, and who is
traditionally referred to by the even more magnificent name of
Rabbi—the rabbi, the master-teacher, the greatest of all. In
its first intention, *Pirke Aboth,* under the name *Aboth,* Fathers,
was one of the tractates of the Mishnah, which is the traditional
Jewish doctrine represented chiefly by rabbinical decisions.
But *Aboth* itself, the last of the tractates, does not deal with
decisions; nor is it what a common English rendering of the
longer title, "Ethics of the Fathers," would seem to imply, for
it is not a system of ethics at all but simply a collection of
maxims and *pensées,* some quite fine, some quite dull, which
praise the life of study and give advice on how to live it.

In speaking of Wordsworth a recollection of boyhood cannot be amiss—my intimacy with this book comes from my
having read it many times in boyhood. It certainly is not the
kind of book a boy is easily drawn to read, and certainly I
did not read it out of piety. On the contrary, indeed: for when

I was supposed to be reading my prayers, very long and in the Hebrew language which I never mastered, I spent the required time reading the English translation of the *Pirke Aboth*, which, although it is not a devotional work, had long ago been thought of as an aid to devotion and included in the prayer-book. It was more attractive to me than psalms, meditations, and supplications; it seemed more humane, and the Fathers had a curious substantiality. Just where they lived I did not know, nor just when, and certainly the rule of life they recommended had a very quaint difference from the life I knew, or, indeed, from any life I wanted to know. Yet they were real, their way of life had the charm of coherence. And when I went back to them, using this time R. Travers Herford's scholarly edition and translation of their sayings,[2] I could feel that my early illicit intimacy with them had prepared the way for my responsiveness to Wordsworth, that between them and him an affinity existed.

But I must at once admit that a large difficulty stands in the way of the affinity I suggest. The *Aboth* is a collection of the sayings of masters of the written word. The ethical life it recommends has for its end the study of Torah, of the law, which alone can give blessedness. So that from the start I am at the disadvantage of trying to make a conjunction between scholars living for the perpetual interpretation of a text and a poet for whom the natural world was at the heart of his doctrine and for whom books were barren leaves. The Rabbis were as suspicious of the natural world as Wordsworth was suspicious of study. That the warning was given at all seems to hint that the Rabbis felt the natural world to be a charm and a temptation, still the *Aboth* does warn us that whoever interrupts his study to observe the beauty of a fine tree or a fine meadow is guilty of sin. And yet I think that it can be said without ex-

---

[2] I have also consulted the edition and translation of the Very Rev. Dr. Joseph H. Hertz, Chief Rabbi of the British Empire, and in my quotations I have drawn upon both versions. Sometimes, when it suited my point, I have combined two versions in a single quotation.

travagance that it is precisely here, where they seem most to differ, that the Rabbis and Wordsworth are most at one. For between the law as the Rabbis understood it and nature as Wordsworth understood that, there is a pregnant similarity.

The Rabbis of the *Aboth* were Pharisees. I shall assume that the long scholarly efforts of Mr. Herford, as well as those of George Foot Moore, have by now made it generally known that the Pharisees were not in actual fact what tradition represents them to have been. They were anything but mere formalists; they were certainly not the hypocrites of popular conception. Here is Mr. Herford's statement of the defining principle of Pharisaism: "The central conception of Pharisaism is Torah, the divine Teaching, the full and inexhaustible revelation which God had made. The knowledge of what was revealed was to be sought, and would be found, in the first instance in the written text of the Pentateuch; but the revelation, the real Torah, was the meaning of what was there written, the meaning as interpreted by all the recognized and accepted methods of the schools, and unfolded in ever greater fullness of detail by successive generations of devoted teachers. The written text of the Pentateuch might be compared to the mouth of a well; the Torah was the water which was drawn from it. He who wished to draw the water must needs go to the well, but there was no limit to the water which was there for him to draw. . . . The study of Torah . . . means therefore much more than the study of the Pentateuch, or even of the whole Scripture, regarded as mere literature, written documents. It means the study of the revelation made through those documents, the divine teaching therein imparted, the divine thought therein disclosed. Apart from the direct intercourse of prayer, the study of Torah was the way of closest approach to God; it might be called the Pharisaic form of the Beatific Vision. To study Torah was, to the devout Pharisee, to 'think God's thoughts after him,' as Kepler said."[3] The

[3] *Pirke Aboth*, ed. with introduction, translation and commentary, third edition, New York, 1945, 14-15.

Rabbis, that is, found sermons in texts, tongues in the running commentary; they conceived failure to lie in supposing that the yellow primrose of a word was a yellow primrose and nothing more.

And Mr. Herford goes on to say that it might be remarked that in the *Aboth* there are very few direct references to God. "This is true," he says, "but it is beside the mark. Wherever Torah is mentioned, there God is implied. He is behind the Torah, the Revealer of what is Revealed."

What I am trying to suggest is that, different as the immediately present objects were in each case, there existed for the Rabbis and for Wordsworth a great object, which is from God and might be said to represent Him as a sort of surrogate, a divine object to which one can be in an intimate passionate relationship, an active relationship—for Wordsworth's "wise passiveness" is of course an activity—which one can, as it were, handle, and in a sense create, drawing from it inexhaustible meaning by desire, intuition, and attention.

And when we turn to the particulars of the *Aboth* we see that the affinity continues. In Jewish tradition the great Hillel has a peculiarly Wordsworthian personality, being the type of gentleness and peace, and having about him a kind of *joy* which has always been found wonderfully attractive; and Hillel said—was, indeed, in the habit of saying: he "used to say"—"If I am not for myself, who, then, is for me? And if I am for myself, what then am I?" Mr. Herford implies that this is a difficult utterance, but it is not difficult for the reader of Wordsworth, who finds the Wordsworthian essence here, the interplay between individualism and the sense of community, between an awareness of the self that must be saved and developed and an awareness that the self is yet fulfilled only in community. How profoundly Wordsworthian too is this saying of Akiba's, which, with so handsome a boldness, handles the problem of fate and free will, of grace and works: "All is foreseen and yet free will is given; and the world is judged by grace and yet all is according to the work."

There are other parallels to be drawn—for example, one finds in the *Aboth* remarks which have a certain wit and daring because they go against the whole tendency of the work in telling us that the multiplication of words is an occasion for sin and that not study but action is the chief thing; one finds the injunction to the scholar to divide his time between study and a trade, presumably in the interest of humility; and the warning that the world must not be too much with him, that getting and spending he lays waste his powers; and the concern with the "ages of man," with the right time in the individual development for each of life's activities. But it is needless to multiply the details of the affinity, which in any case must not be insisted on too far. All that I want to suggest is the community of ideal and sensibility between the *Aboth* and the canon of Wordsworth's work—the passionate contemplation and experience of the great object which is proximate to Deity; then the plain living that goes with the high thinking, the desire for the humble life and the discharge of duty; and last, but not least important, a certain insouciant acquiescence in the anomalies of the moral order of the universe, a respectful indifference to, or a graceful surrender before, the mysteries of the moral relation of God to man.

This last element as it is expressed by Akiba's *pensée* has, I think, its connection with something in the *Aboth* which for me is definitive of its quality. Actually it is something not in the *Aboth* but left out—we find in the tractate no implication of spiritual struggle. We find the energy of assiduity but not the energy of resistance. We hear about sin, but we do not hear about the sinful nature of man. Man in the *Aboth* guards against sin but he does not struggle against it, and of evil we hear nothing at all. When we have observed this it is natural to observe next that there is no mention in the *Aboth* of courage or heroism. In our culture we connect the notion of courage or heroism with the religious life. We conceive of the perpetual enemy within and the perpetual enemy without which must be "withstood," "overcome," "conquered"—the language of religion and the language of fighting are in our culture assimilated to each other. Not so in the *Aboth*. The enemy within seems not to be conceived of at all. The enemy without is never mentioned, although the *Aboth* was compiled after the Dispersion, after the temple and the nation had been destroyed, with what heroism in the face of suffering we know from Josephus. Of the men whose words are cited, many met martyrdom for their religion, and the martyrology records their calm and fortitude in torture and death; of Akiba it records his heroic joy. And yet in their maxims they never speak of courage.

As much as anything else in my boyhood experience of the *Aboth* it was this that fascinated me. It also repelled me. It had the double effect because it went so clearly against the militancy of spirit which in our culture is normally assumed. And even now as I consider this indifference to heroism, I have the old ambiguous response to it, so that I think I can understand the feelings that readers have when they encounter something similar in Wordsworth. For there is indeed something similar in Wordsworth. It is what Matthew Arnold notes when in the *Memorial Verses* he compares Wordsworth with Byron, who was for Arnold the embodiment of militancy of spirit. Arnold said of Wordsworth that part of his peculiar value to us arose from his indifference to "man's fiery might," to the Byronic courage in fronting human destiny.

> The cloud of mortal destiny,
> Others will front it fearlessly—
> But who, like him, will put it by?

Arnold certainly did not mean that Wordsworth lacked courage or took no account of it. He liked nothing better, indeed, than to recite examples of courage, but the Wordsworthian courage is different in kind from the Byronic. For one thing, it is never aware of itself, it is scarcely personal. It is the courage of mute, insensate things, and is often poetically associated with these things, with rocks and stones and trees, or with stars. Michael on his hilltop, whose character is defined by the light of his cottage, which was called "The Evening Star," and by the stones of his sheepfold; or the Leech Gatherer, who is like some old, great rock; or Margaret, who, like a tree, endured as long as she might after she was blasted. Of the Lesser Celandine it is said that its fortitude is neither its courage nor its choice but its necessity in being old, and the same thing is to be said of all of Wordsworth's exemplars of courage: they endure because they are what they are, and we might almost say that they survive out of a kind of biological faith, which is not the less human because it is nearly an animal or vegetable faith; and, indeed, as I have suggested, it is sometimes nearly mineral. Even the Happy Warrior, the man in arms, derives his courage not from his militancy of spirit but from his calm submission to the law of things.

In Wordsworth's vision of life, then, the element of quietude approaches passivity, even insentience, and the dizzy raptures of youth have their issue in the elemental existence of which I have spoken. The scholars of the *Aboth* certainly had no such notion; they lived for intellectual sentience. But where the scholars and Wordsworth are at one is in the quietism, which is not in the least a negation of life, but on the contrary an affirmation of life so complete that it needed no saying. To the Rabbis, as I read them, there life was, unquestionable because committed to a divine object. There life was—in our view rather stuffy and airless, or circumscribed and thin, but very intense and absolutely and utterly real, not needing to be affirmed by force or assertion, real because the object of its regard was unquestioned and because that object was unquestionably more important than the individual persons who regarded it and lived by it. To Wordsworth, as I read him, a similar thing was true in its own way. Much as he loved to affirm the dizzy raptures of sentience, of the ear and the eye and the mind, he also loved to move down the scale of being,

142

to say that when the spirit was sealed by slumber, was without motion and force, when it was like a rock or a stone or a
tree, not hearing or seeing and passive in the cosmic motion,
that even then, or especially then, existence was blessed.

Now nothing could be further from the tendency of our
culture than this Wordsworthian attitude or quality of feeling.
We can say in general that our culture is committed to nothing
so much as sentience and activity, to motion and force, and
that with us the basis of spiritual prestige is some form of
violence directed toward others or toward ourselves. An example comes conveniently to hand in T. S. Eliot's explanation of
the decline of Wordsworth's genius from its greatness to what
Mr. Eliot calls the "still sad music of infirmity." Wordsworth,
says Mr. Eliot, suffered from the lack of an eagle—that eagle
which André Gide's Prometheus says is necessary for the successful spiritual or poetic life: *"Il faut avoir un aigle."*[4] This
fierce but validating bird, this *aigle obligatoire,* suggests the
status of the feral and the violent in our literature. Nothing is
better established in our literary life than the knowledge that
the tigers of wrath are better than the horses of instruction.
We have been taught that we must give our partisanship to
the fierce bulls in the ring rather than to the worn, patient,
disembowelled horses. Or in the matter of horses themselves,
we have been taught to prefer those of Plato's chariot which
are black and wild to those which are white. We do not, to be
sure, live in the fashion of the beasts we admire in our literary
lives—the discrepancy is much to the point—but we cherish
them as representing something that we all seem to seek. They
are the emblems of that *charisma*—to borrow a word which
the sociologists have borrowed from the theologians—which is
the hot, direct relationship with godhead, or with the sources
of life upon which depend our notions of what I have called
spiritual prestige.

[4] "Wordsworth and Coleridge," *The Use of Poetry and the Use of
Criticism,* Cambridge, Mass., 1933, 60.

At every point in our culture we find the predilection which makes it impossible for most readers to accept Wordsworth. It is the predilection for the powerful, the fierce, the assertive, the personally heroic. There is manifest everywhere in our literature the search for a sort of personal, private *charisma*, the desire for the acquisition of *mana*. We find it in the liberal-bourgeois admiration of the novels of Thomas Wolfe and of Theodore Dreiser. On a somewhat lower intellectual level we find it in the popularity of the curious demonism of that curious underground work, *The Fountainhead*. On a higher intellectual level we find it in the response to certain aspects of Yeats and Lawrence, whose celebration of force will suggest a standard element in contemporary literature. It appears in our politics, for quite apart from what we actually *do* about politics, when we mix it up with our sensibility, we are convinced in our hearts that politics should be ultimate and absolute, that, at the behest of the pure, perfect, magical vision, we should finish up things once and for all. We find it in our religion, or in our conception of religion—to most intellectuals the violence of Dostoievski represents the natural form of the religious life; and although some years ago Mr. Eliot reprobated Lawrence, in the name of religion, for his addiction to this characteristic violence, yet for Mr. Eliot the equally violent Baudelaire is pre-eminently a Christian poet.

I cannot give a better description of the quality of our literature I am concerned with than by quoting the characterization of it which Richard Chase found occasion to make in the course of a review of a notable English scholar, Professor Willey.[5] It is relevant to remark that Professor Willey deals with the nineteenth century from the point of view of the Anglican form of Christianity, and Mr. Chase is commenting on Professor Willey's hostility to a certain Victorian figure who, in any discussion of Wordsworth, must inevitably be in

[5] *Nineteenth Century Studies: Coleridge to Matthew Arnold*, London, 1949.

our minds—John Stuart Mill: his name seems very queer and shocking when it is spoken together with the names of the headlong figures of modern literature. "Among the Victorians," says Mr. Chase, "it is Mill who tests the modern mind, and in relation to him at least two of its weaknesses come quickly to light. The first is its morose desire for dogmatic certainty. The second is its hyperaesthesia: its feeling that no thought is permissible except an extreme thought; that every idea must be directly emblematic of concentration camps, alienation, madness, hell, history, and God; that every word must bristle and explode with the magic potency of our plight."[6]

I must be careful not to seem to speak, as certainly Mr. Chase is not speaking, against the sense of urgency and immediacy, or against power; and certainly not against the great, sad figures of modern literature. Nor would I be taken to mean that the Wordsworthian way of feeling is the whole desideratum of the emotional life. We all know that there is an extension of the Wordsworthian feeling that we dread. When in *The Excursion* the Wanderer and the Poet and the Pastor sit upon the gravestones and tell sad stories of the deaths of other mild old men for the benefit of the Solitary, who has had his fling at life and is understandably a little bitter, we know that something wrong is being done to us; we long for the winding of a horn or the drawing of a sword, we want someone to dash in on a horse—I think we want exactly a stallion. For there can be no doubt about it, Wordsworth at the extreme or perversion of himself carries the element of quietude to the denial of sexuality; and perhaps at all times he implies a non-sexuality. And this is eventually what makes the *Aboth* seem quaint and oppressive, what, I suppose, makes a modern reader uneasy under any of the philosophies which urge us to the contemplation of a unitary reality which is described as being disturbed and destroyed by the desires. Whether it be the Torah of the *Aboth,* or the cosmos of Marcus Aurelius, or the nature of

[6] *The Nation,* April 8, 1950, 330.

Spinoza or of Wordsworth, it depends upon the suppression not only of the sexual emotions but also of the qualities that are associated with sexuality: high-heartedness, self-assertiveness, wit, creative innovation.

But now, when we have touched upon the Wordsworthian quality which is very close to *apatheia,* let us remember what great particular thing it was that Wordsworth accomplished. Matthew Arnold's statement cannot be bettered. In a wintry clime, in an iron time, Wordsworth taught us to feel. What a statement to make, what a thing to say! What it implies of our culture for some two centuries, of the situation in the general life which has been expressed by the most sensitive observers as the inability to experience the emotions which have traditionally been associated with simply being human! The instruction in the emotions which Arnold says was Wordsworth's characteristic work was certainly not completed by Wordsworth. It has been taken up by almost every notable writer of our own day. There is scarcely a contemporary writer who has not addressed himself to the feelings as if they were a problem, who has not tried to go back to roots and sources in order to reconstitute the strength of the emotions. They do so, to be sure, under a necessity somewhat different from Wordsworth's, and this necessity makes it seem to them appropriate that, with Byron, they assert fiery life. (Blake more aptly suggests the quality of their militancy, but I stay with the terms of Arnold's opposition.) It is not hard to understand this. Their fierce animals are partly political animals in that sense of the word political which has to do with the quality of being that a man is permitted to have. Their beasts, wrong-headed, cruel, or limited in understanding as beasts often are, have been created to assert some of the personal qualities that are associated with an older, a presumably freer and more personally aristocratic time. As such we must regard them with ambivalence. A certain sliced-off ear which is an object of pleasure to Yeats, a certain kick given by an employer to his employee

146

which wins approval from Lawrence—these repel us and remind us of some of the actual consequences of the *charisma*
and *mana* that we desire. Yet we know that this violence can,
in other aspects, serve to stand against an extreme fate of
which we are all conscious. We really know in our time what
the death of the word can be—for that knowledge we have only
to read an account of contemporary Russian literature. We
really know now what the death of the spirit means; we have
seen it overtake whole peoples. And we understand that the
violent animals are intended to protect us from being the gored
or work-destroyed horse, or the ox, or the plucked and de-
voured goose.

This we must be aware of, and yet at the same time we cannot help seeing that the extreme violence and assertiveness
of the great fierce beasts go along with the most profound
depression of spirits, along with boredom, *ennui, noia, acedia.*
The extremity of the one leads to the extremity of the other,
and it doesn't much matter from which you start—the oscilla-
tion must be perpetual. What Wordsworth knew—and said,
for he had his comment to make on the literature of violence—
is that life does not have to be justified and feeling affirmed by
that which is violent, or by that which is proud: the meanest
flower is enough. What he asserted was the justification of life
where no pride and fierceness is. He laid us, Arnold said, on
the lap of earth—reminded us, that is, of the infant existence
before the social pride had put its mark on us. He groped, not
always sure of his direction but always sure of his intention,
toward the images of the extremity of the will that would
destroy the roots of life, and the will itself. If we bring it up
against him that he negated some of these very roots, for instance the sexual ones, may it not be answered that perhaps
they exactly needed to be negated for a time, so charged were
they, and still are, with the tensions of the will?

Perhaps nothing could better summarize our passion for the
heroic ultimate than a recent incident of our literature of which

everyone seems to be aware. I refer to Mr. Eliot's description in *The Cocktail Party* of the two virtuous ways of life, that of daily, habitual routine—Wordsworth was particularly interested in it—and that of spiritual heroism. The two ways, Mr. Eliot tells us, are of equal value, the way of the saint is not better than that of the common householder. Yet when it comes to describing the life of "the common routine," Mr. Eliot says this of those who elect it: that they

> Learn to avoid excessive expectation,
> Become tolerant of themselves and others,
> Giving and taking, in the usual actions
> What there is to give and take. They do not repine;
> And are contented with the morning that separates
> And with the evening that brings together
> For casual talk before the fire
> Two people who know that they do not understand each
>   other,
> Breeding children whom they do not understand
> And who will never understand them.

Well, few of us will want to say much for the life of the common routine, the life without an eagle, yet we know we can say more than this. We know that it is both more wonderful and more terrible than Mr. Eliot says it is, having its moments of unbearable pain and its moments of glory—I use the Wordsworthian word with intention. And this failure of Mr. Eliot's to conceive the pains and glories of the habitual life is typical of modern literature since, say, Tolstoy. We are drawn to the violence of extremity. In our hearts we subscribe to the belief that the more sin the more grace, or at any rate the more life. We are in love, at least in our literature, with the fantasy of death—perhaps this is not new and we now but intensify what is indigenous in our culture. Death and suffering, when we read, are our only means of testing the actuality

148

of life; and it is impossible for us to make real the image of love unless death attend it.

Perhaps this is in the nature of life as Western culture has long been, and will continue to be, fated to see it: which may also be to say that this is in the nature of life. Perhaps it is inescapable that for us the word *tragic* must be the ultimate recommendation of a sense of life. But we, when we use the word, barely mean it, we mean something like violent and conclusive; we mean death: for us tragedy is the violent, conclusive gesture of dying. And just here lies a paradox and our point. For it is precisely the true awareness of what Wordsworth called common life, and even of common life as it exists at a very low level of consciousness, pride, and assertiveness, that validates heroism and tragedy. If we ask why the martyrdom which Mr. Eliot presents in his play seems to us somewhat factitious, however much we may respect the intention for which it was conceived, must we not answer that this is because it is presented in a system of feeling which sets very little store by the life of the common routine? And this seems to be borne out by the emphasis which is put on the peculiar horror of the death, as if only by an extremity of pain could we be made to realize that a life has been sacrificed—or, indeed, has been lived.

Wordsworth's incapacity for tragedy has often been remarked on, and accurately enough. Yet we cannot conclude that Wordsworth's relation to tragedy is wholly negative. The possibility of tragic art in any honorific sense of the word depends primarily upon the worth we ascribe not to dying but to living, and to living in the common routine. The Homeric tragedy, for example, exists in its power by reason of the pathos, which the poet is at pains to bring before us again and again, of young men dying, of not seeing ever again the trees of their native farmsteads, of not being admired and indulged by their parents, of not being permitted to live out the common routine. The tragic hero, Achilles, becomes a tragic hero

149

exactly because he has made choice to give up the life of the common routine which all his comrades yearn for, and the pathos of his particular situation becomes the great thing it is because of the respondent pathos of Hector and Priam, the pathos of the family and the common routine, which we understand less and less and find ourselves more and more uncomfortable with. And I think it can be shown that every tragic literature owes its power to captivate us to the high esteem in which it holds the common routine, the elemental *given* of biology. So that although Wordsworth is indeed far from tragic art, we can say that he sought to nourish its very germ.

It has not been my intention to make a separation between Wordsworth and the literature of our time. The separation cannot, indeed, be made really to exist. There never was, I believe, a secular literature which so massively and so explicitly as ours directed itself to the spiritual life, for good or bad carrying the problems of life and death into the marketplace: Alexandria was nothing to us when it comes to a theological population. In this movement of secular exploration of the spirit Wordsworth was a founding father. And not merely because of his general preoccupation is Wordsworth part of modern literature. He initiated the attack on the problem that has involved the energies of a main part of modern literature, the problem of affectlessness, of loss of feeling and of humanness, under which we subsume all the details of our modern spiritual plight. Even in that one decisive element of his work which I have isolated to distinguish him from the tendency of contemporary literature, he has been followed as well as departed from. For when we have taken account of all that is feral and fierce and consciously heroic and charismatic in our literature, we must yet recognize how strong, if still subaltern, is the impulse to find the validation of life in its common, elemental, instinctual roots, in its enduring humility. Not only Faulkner's Negroes, of whom it is said, as it is so often said of people by Wordsworth, *they endured,* but Faulkner's many images of the significance of elemental existence; the curious, quiet dignity of Hemingway's waiters; Joyce's paternal dreamer and Joyce's preference for Bloom over Dedalus; even Dreiser's Jennie Gerhardt; Lawrence's representation of people whose pride is only that of plants and animals —out of the characteristic violence these and others come movingly to mind.

In one other respect Wordsworth is of our time—he taught us not only to feel but to remember. What role the art of memory has played in our literature needs scarcely to be spoken of. The instances of its use will occur to everyone; they are so numerous as to make an endemic condition of our thought and to suggest that something like a mutation in the nature of man has taken place. But at the same time that we observe this flowering of the faculty of memory and relate it to the great nineteenth-century movement in the study of history and to modern theories of growth and development, we must observe as well the tendency of our democratic culture to wish to forget. We of the universities can be especially aware of this tendency. We feel the pressure upon us to prove our usefulness by displaying our sense of the immediately contemporary and our power over it, and we know that the mandate of the contemporary and the instrumental brings with it the strong implication that the least useful thing the universities can do is to continue their old characteristic work of conservation, of keeping alive, in some part of the social mind, the culture of the past.

It is indeed very difficult to demonstrate that this is truly a socially useful work, yet Wordsworth taught us that some truth and strength were to be gained for the personal life by binding our days together, and we may well suppose that the same thing may be said of the communal life. I have noted the wide discrepancy that exists between the opinion of Wordsworth that is held by the modern world and the opinion that is expressed by the universities in commemorations like this one. It seems worth saying that in consenting to this discrepancy, in maintaining our own opinion, in preserving and finding interesting a spirit that the world at this moment thinks dead and done with, we do something to fulfill one of the essential functions of the university in our society.

WORDSWORTH'S RELIGION

BY WILLARD L. SPERRY

I will lift up mine eyes unto the hills, from whence cometh my help.

Psalms, CXXXI.1

Hail to you

Moors, mountains, headlands, and ye hollow vales, . . .

Powers of my native region!

The Prelude, VIII. 215-18

IT WILL be well, in considering Wordsworth's religion, to approach the subject by the *via negativa,* and thus to say what it was not. Conventional critics have often referred to Wordsworth's religion as a kind of mild pantheism and dismissed it as such. The last two lines of the Lucy poems have a pantheistic ring:

> Rolled round in earth's diurnal course,
> With rocks, and stones, and trees.

But whatever sort of believer Wordsworth was, he was not a pantheist. Pantheism is amoral; it does not recognize the existence of evil and therefore does not have to wrestle with the problem of evil. Not so with Wordsworth. He was burdened with the mystery and the heavy and the weary weight of all this unintelligible world. He felt the general sorrow of mankind. He heard the still, sad music of humanity. He saw the race moving in a mighty caravan of pain. In particular he was aware of man's inhumanity to man. All this lies far apart from pantheism.

Wordsworth was not a social mystic. It is true that he refers constantly to the common or general heart of man. He boldly affirmed that

153

there is
One great society alone on earth:
The noble Living and the noble Dead.[1]

But such ideas are little more than abstractions. Concretely, and in spite of his protestation that when he went to France his heart was given to the people, Wordsworth was wholly without that sense of identity with all sorts and conditions of men which we find, for instance, in Walt Whitman or in Tolstoy. He could make nothing of London. It was a sealed book to him; its crowds only intensified his loneliness. It was a monstrous, meaningless ant-hill on the plain of the world. The only time he felt able to grasp the city of London was when he saw it from Westminster Bridge in early dawn, its houses asleep and its mighty heart lying still. So in France, he was from first to last an alien and an onlooker. His professed identification with the people of the Revolution resolved itself into philosophical conversations with his friend Beaupuy along the banks of the Loire.

Many persons would rest the case for the poet's religion on the famous *Ode on Intimations of Immortality*. He apparently believed in the pre-existence of the soul and he certainly believed in the immortality of the soul. But it should be pointed out that the idea of immortality is in most religions a corollary of a prior belief in God. Of itself it does not satisfy the basic conception of religion, which is that of some kind of correspondence with a reality other than the soul.

It is the custom of many commentators to identify Wordsworth's religion with the decorous High-Church Anglicanism to which he turned in his rather conventional Tory days. The *Ecclesiastical Sonnets* may seem to give some weight to this appraisal of the facts. But these sonnets, though they contain occasional fine lines, instinct with piety, are primarily a set of versified studies in English church history. It is noticeable

[1] *The Prelude* (1850), XI, 393-5.

154

that when Wordsworth is in a church he is usually studying the memorials on the walls, rather than reading the Prayer Book. More often we find him wandering around the church-yard outside, brooding over the gravestones. Wordsworth undoubtedly had a deep feeling for the Church of England, but this was a feeling for the one institution above all others, more even than the state, which guaranteed to him the grounds of his faith in the continuity and survival of a homely English culture as a whole.

It has been suggested that Wordsworth's religion, or perhaps his lack of religion, crystallized as a guilt feeling over the affair with Annette. Psychoanalytically minded critics have found here the secret of his waning poetic powers over the last forty years of his life. This line of argument fails to convince me. I find it impossible, for instance, to believe that a man who was harried by a bad conscience would ever have written *It is a beauteous evening, calm and free,* in which his illegitimate daughter is incidentally addressed as "Dear Child! dear Girl! that walkest with me here." What really occupied Wordsworth's mind that evening was the sunset over Calais beach, not a secret guilt feeling over his own youthful indiscretion. The "Dear Child" was little more than a bit of stage property, not an occasion for poignant remorse.

Having deleted these false leads, we are now free to consider the subject of Wordsworth's religion in its own terms. I venture to suggest as a key to our problem a few familiar words from Alfred North Whitehead: "The great religious conceptions which haunt the imaginations of civilized mankind are scenes of solitariness. . . . Thus religion is solitariness; and if you are never solitary, you are never religious. . . . Religion is what the individual does with his own solitariness. It runs through three stages. . . . It is the transition from God the void to God the enemy, and from God the enemy to God the companion."[2]

[2] *Religion in the Making,* New York, 1926, 16-19.

If this account of the matter is true, there is no sourcebook in all English literature, even its conventionally religious literature, by which it may be verified so fully as in Wordsworth's poems. In his essay on Wordsworth, in the *Oxford Lectures on Poetry*, Professor A. C. Bradley says that Wordsworth is "preeminently the poet of solitude." The importance of this accurate observation should not be overlooked. The words "solitary," "solitude," "alone," "lonely" are shot as a woof through the whole long warp of Wordsworth's verse. Go through your own copy of the poems and underline those words, as I have done in my copy. The solitary sheep, the lonely tarn, the single shepherd seen on the skyline, the solitary tree, the souls of lonely places, the poet himself wandering lonely as a cloud—all these are so constant as to seem mere verbal tags with Wordsworth. Such references represent, however, his deeper mental second nature, and were never literary artifices.

I can think of only two passages in English literature which give us to the same degree scenes of solitariness which haunt the imagination and to this extent stir the imagination. They are both by Thomas Hardy: one, the description of Egdon Heath at night in the opening chapter of *The Return of the Native*; the other, the equally eerie account of Stonehenge as Tess of the D'Urbervilles stumbles on it at midnight. The latter reference to Stonehenge is, indeed, paralleled by a passage in Wordsworth's own verse. In any case there is no phrase in all the poems more authentically Wordsworthian than that in *Michael*, which describes the old man as having been "alone amid the heart of many thousand mists." In writing that line, Wordsworth was autobiographical.

The aftermath of this initial experience of solitariness follows, in Wordsworth, the logic of Whitehead's thought. The first reaction is that to God-the-void. The poet stresses the self-sufficing power of solitude in his earlier experiences; he felt so safe and so secure in his solitariness. The surrounding world was vacant, empty, unresponsive. There hung over his mind a sense of blank desertion. Yet this very emptiness was a challenge. One cannot fail to notice the importance of the idea of the echo in his early verse. True, it was only his own voice returning to him, but that at least was returned. There was some kind of comeback from the outer world. So, also, with his boyish hootings at the owls in the attempt to get them to hoot back, he plainly wanted some response to redeem or supplement his intense feeling of loneliness.

There is no doubt that, in the terms of his relation to nature, the poet passed through a period in which he was aware of God-the-enemy. The famous passages in *The Prelude* about skating and rowing reflect an uneasy and apprehensive sense of a world which was wholly alien to himself, if not potentially hostile. He felt himself surrounded by

> huge and mighty forms, that do not live
> Like living men.

In such experiences he was, in his own words,

> more like a man
> Flying from something that he dreads than one
> Who sought the thing he loved.[3]

This sense of the antipathetic aspects of the natural world is written into his accounts of the Alps, where man is found suffering among awful powers and forms.

Wordsworth did not find God-the-companion until his eventual return to the Lake District. He found that God in the terms of the natural world. There may be in his verse a residual heritage from some "Pagan suckled in a creed outworn," but there is far more than that. It has been much the custom of modern criticism to dismiss Wordsworth's feeling for God in nature as a pleasant fancy denied us moderns because of our awareness of the bestiality and cruelty of nature. H. G. Wells has said that being laid on the lap of nature is like cuddling up to a Siberian tiger. Aldous Huxley is more explicit. He says that

---

[3] *Tintern Abbey*, 70-2.

Wordsworth's love of nature is possible only for those who live in thoroughly domesticated areas of the natural world, and that a voyage through the venomous and vicious tropics would have disabused the poet of his too easy and comfortable faith.[4]

One must remember that Wordsworth antedated the time when the dogma of the struggle for existence raised for our generation a whole set of ethical problems which the poet's own generation was never called upon to face. We cannot criticize him for not anticipating, for instance, the issues which Thomas Huxley discussed in his famous Romanes Lecture on *Evolution and Ethics*. Wordsworth's feeling for nature was still that of the Psalmist, not that of the modern biologist. Nor can we blame him if, in maturity, he deliberately decided to follow the injunction of the book of *Proverbs* to "rejoice in the habitable parts of God's earth." His instinct was probably more nearly right than the masochistic tendency of the modern mind to torture itself by trying to live in uninhabitable parts of the total scene in nature and history. For, as in nature Wordsworth found the higher Alps uninhabitable, so, in history, he found the Reign of Terror uninhabitable.

In any case, it is in the detailed descriptions of his mature relation to nature as being a revelation of God-the-companion that we come to the core of Wordsworth's religion. Here and there one gets traces of the Stoic doctrine of the *Logos*, most conspicuously perhaps in the lines of *Tintern Abbey* which speak of

> A motion and a spirit, that impels
> All thinking things, all objects of all thought,
> And rolls through all things.

But the point to notice is this—Wordsworth never actually identifies the thinker and the object of his thought. His poetry as a whole is a witness to the way in which

[4] "Wordsworth in the Tropics," *Do What You Will*, New York, 1930, 123-39.

> the individual Mind
> . . . to the external World
> Is fitted:—and how exquisitely, too—. . .
> The external World is fitted to the Mind.[5]

He was always scrupulous

> to keep
> In wholesome separation the two natures,
> The one that feels, the other that observes.[6]

He tried to preserve

> A balance, an ennobling interchange
> Of action from without and from within;
> The excellence, pure function, and best power
> Both of the object seen, and eye that sees.[7]

He counselled a wise passiveness, a responsiveness to things that of themselves do come, a heart that watches and receives. But he never lapsed into sheer quietism. Though he realized that he had perhaps been at times too subservient to external things, nevertheless

> an auxiliar light
> Came from my mind, which on the setting sun
> Bestowed new splendour.[8]

Thus the light that never was on land or sea came from his own imagination, and he felt himself,

> Like a lone shepherd on a promontory
> Who lacking occupation looks far forth
> Into the boundless sea, and rather makes
> Than finds what he beholds.[9]

Passages to this effect can be multiplied indefinitely from *The Prelude* and *The Excursion*. They remain in English verse, and indeed in all our letters, an unmatched witness to the

[5] Conclusion to *The Recluse*, I, 63-8.
[6] *The Prelude* (1850), XIV, 345-7.   [7] *Ibid.*, XIII, 375-8.
[8] *Ibid.*, II, 368-70.   [9] *Ibid.*, III, 516-19.

159

duality of the religious consciousness, a consciousness of self
and a consciousness of God, each independent of the other,
yet interdependent and in an intimate mutual relationship. The
terms of that relationship may be those of man to nature, but
the basic and elemental quality of all religious experience is
there. Let it be said, in passing, that Wordsworth never avoided
the word "God." He used it simply and in good faith, even
though his God was primarily "Nature's God." However deeply
interfused in the processes of nature the poet may have felt
God to be, his doctrine of God made full place for the divine
transcendence, as well as immanence. Thus he speaks of

the one
Surpassing Life, which out of space and time,
Nor touched by welterings of passion, is
And hath the name of God.[10]

I sometimes think that of all the ascriptions to God which man
has coined none is more moving than the poet's reference to
God as an "Eternity of Thought."

Two brief comments on Wordsworth's religion remain to
be made. For practical purposes it is the office of religion to
unify our life, to prevent its being shattered into meaningless
fragments. The soul's identity, as Emily Dickinson knew, is a
hound that only too easily slips its leash. In an age when exis-
tentialism can only give to our experience the name of Legion,
it is worth while to go back to Wordsworth and live over with
him his struggle to preserve the soul's identity in the terms
of a consistent, coherent, consecutive self-consciousness. He
brought back with him to the Lake District the remnants of
a life which had been violently fragmented. There was little
coherence and less continuity in the experiences through which
he had passed. He concedes that he might possibly have lin-
gered on in France to perish with his revolutionary friends,

[10] *The Prelude* (1805-6), vi, 154-7.

A poor mistaken and bewildered offering,—
Should to the breast of Nature have gone back,
With all my resolutions, all my hopes.[11]

But Wordsworth was not a Byron, and it would have been a fruitless pose for him to have affected a Byronic mood and role. His return to England may seem unheroic, but the instinct which prompted it was sound. He was able, in retrospect, to understand how

all
The terrors, pains, and early miseries,
Regrets, vexations, lassitudes interfused
Within my mind, should e'er have borne a part,
And that a needful part, in making up
The calm existence that is mine when I
Am worthy of myself.[12]

All this is written into the few lines about the rainbow, which is not a poem about a rainbow at all, rather about self-consciousness and the means by which man's days may be bound each to each by natural piety. Wordsworth won that victory by hard self-discipline and much reflection, and his ability to do so is an encouragement to all those who today are hagridden by the specter of schizophrenia, or seduced by the existentialists.

Finally, Wordsworth's religion, as Leslie Stephen has said, gave to the poet the power to transmute his agonizing sorrows. He imputes the spiritual tragedy and failure of one of his characters in *The Excursion* to the lack of that power. The ethical, and perhaps the religious, timeliness of Wordsworth's more serious verse lies in the fact that we too have passed through an era not unlike that in which he lived. We have known the loss of faith in social man which has followed the collapse of a premature utopianism. The major moral peril of our time is vested in a widespread pessimism which only too easily lapses

---

[11] *The Prelude* (1850), x, 231-3.   [12] *Ibid.*, i, 344-50.

into cynicism. Wordsworth knew that peril only too well, but
he prevailed over it. He arrived, with a great price, at a

> central peace, subsisting at the heart
> Of endless agitation.

He won that confidence by giving substance to his hope that
his life might

> Express the image of a better time,
> More wise desires, and simpler manners.

His regimen for so doing is by no means out of date. And any
man who can recover and reaffirm his deep feeling for some
ultimate and central peace at the heart of the endless agitation
of our day will be one of the helpers of humanity, even though
his help is not given in the terms of politics or economics. It
is the quality of such confidence which matters, not its particular formulation.

At times it seems as though the happy ending of the Wordsworth epic is a little too bland, and perhaps rather too facile.
The endless agitation of these present years may seem to deny
us the poet's

> cheerful faith, that all which we behold
> Is full of blessings.

It should be remembered that this faith was not an inference
from immediate facts; it was a confidence grounded in the
poet's mature convictions as to the witness of nature to the
character of God.

Just at the time that Wordsworth died, in April 1850, Matthew Arnold asked

> But where will Europe's latter hour
> Again find Wordsworth's healing power?

For a hundred years there has never been any single convinc-
ing answer to that question, which is far more imperative

today than it was a century ago. One has to go back to the poet
himself, to recover if possible his faith in

> That secret spirit of humanity
> Which, 'mid the calm oblivious tendencies
> Of nature, 'mid her plants, and weeds, and flowers,
> And silent overgrowings, still survived.[13]

In these days when our horizon is darkened by the menace
of incredible desolation which may be spread over the face
of our earth, as a final act in the tragedy of man's inhumanity
to man, my own mind often harks back to an almost prophetic
passage in *The Prelude* in which Wordsworth's own feeling
for exultations, agonies and love and man's unconquerable
mind finds confident voice:

> A thought is with me sometimes, and I say,—
> Should the whole frame of earth by inward throes
> Be wrenched, or fire come down from far to scorch
> Her pleasant habitations, and dry up
> Old Ocean, in his bed left singed and bare,
> Yet would the living Presence still subsist
> Victorious, and composure would ensue,
> And kindlings like the morning—presage sure
> Of day returning and of life revived.

[13] *The Excursion,* I, 927-30.

INDEX OF PERSONS AND TITLES

14323